AN AMERICAN JOURNEY

AN AMERICAN JOURNEY

BY

JOHN L. PALUSZEK

American Ethnic Press

New York, New York

For permission or information on purchase of copies, write American Ethnic Press, P.O. Box 1994, Grand Central Station, New York, New York 10163.

Library of Congress Cataloging in Publication Data
Catalog Card No.: 81–65201
Paluszek, John
   An American Journey
NY: American Ethnic Press
135 p.
8103   810113

International Standard Book Number (ISBN) 0–9605766–0–6

This book is dedicated to

My Father

who believed so deeply in America
that he left everything he had in the old country
to build a new life here—
and in doing so made America better still.

ACKNOWLEDGMENT

I'm indebted to the Polish American Museum Foundation, Port Washington, L.I., for the assistance I received from Foundation members and from its archives during the development of this book.

John L. Paluszek
January, 1981

CONTENTS

INTRODUCTION

September 1, 1980: Labor Day, U.S.A. For nearly one hundred years this day has been set aside as a tribute to the American worker. Throughout the land, as in years before, public officials, civic leaders and union officers mounted flag-draped platforms in public squares and parks to extoll the virtues of the working class. Speeches heralding the heroic contributions of working men and women to the advancement of our society were the order of the day.

Almost half a world away, it was a special day in Poland, too. But for different reasons. On September 1 forty-one years ago, German invaders violated Polish frontiers and marched on its capital. Warsaw fell on September 27, 1939 following a twenty-day siege during which thousands of its brave defenders perished and much of the city was reduced to rubble. The anniversary of the invasion is observed with solemn ceremonies in Poland. Now it will be remembered for still another reason. On September 1, 1980 hundreds of thousands of Polish workers returned to their jobs in shipyards and factories after a bloodless revolt to win economic, political and social reforms from their government, reforms without precedent under a communist system.

For almost three weeks the world watched breathlessly as Polish workers courageously defied all constituted authority to demand basic freedoms guaranteed by their own Constitution and by the Final Act of the Conference on Security and Cooperation in Europe, which the Polish Government signed at Helsinki, August 1, 1975. The freedom that the government granted with the greatest reluctance, and then only with severe restrictions, was the one on which Labor Day is based: the right to form free and independent trade unions.

It was not the first time that Poles had demonstrated their love of freedom and basic human rights. The freedom of the Polish spirit was dramatically expressed in the Polish Constitution of May 3, 1791, just a few years before Poland was partitioned between its strong and greedy neighbors, disappearing as a state for more than a century, to be reborn after World War I following the Treaty of Versailles and the victory of Polish troops over the Soviet Army in 1920. A generation later, the Polish spirit survived yet another war with its wanton destruction and with millions of its citizens the victims of Nazi genocide, the nation rising like a Phoenix from the smoldering ashes of its beautiful capital.

This is a book about the Polish spirit, embodied in that nation's people and their descendants, even in foreign lands. This is a book about the spirit of Mikolaj Kopernik, known as Copernicus to the world; Casimir

Pulaski; Thaddeus Kosciuszko; Marie Sklodowska-Curie; Ignace Jan Paderewski; Adam Mickiewicz, and thousands of other Poles who gained world reknown over the centuries of recorded history in their search for truth, beauty, justice, freedom and equality. They gave the world an example of determination, tenacity and love of life, a legacy inherited by some twelve million Americans from their ancestors of Polish origin.

This is a book about the loyalty of Poland and its people to their God and to the Catholic church, which is so much a part of the national spirit as to be inseparable from it. For over one thousand years, the faith of the Polish people has been their strength and inspiration. It is this faith which has made it possible for the nation to survive every form of religious persecution and suppression. This intense faith became a new source of joy in October, 1978 when Karol Cardinal Wojtyla, the Bishop of Cracow, was selected to head the Catholic church, the first non-Italian Pope in over four hundred years, and the first ever to be called to Rome from a country whose government is based on principles which deny the very existence of God. Polish hearts swelled with pride and Americans of Polish descent found new reason to proclaim their ethnicity.

A year and a half later, when Pope John Paul II visited his native land, hundreds of thousands of his fellow countrymen greeted him with unbounded enthusiasm at every stopover. Imagine, a Pole had achieved the highest pinnacle in the worldwide and eternal church!

In his sermons, the Pope, once a factory worker himself, spoke of the world of work, the importance of the worker, and the dignity of human labor. And in August, 1980 the leader of the Strike Committee signed the agreement in which the communist government of Poland acceded to the workers' principal demands with a pen bearing the image of the Pope from Poland.

This is a book about the ties between two nations, strengthened by a hundred years of emigration from the old country to the new. The first Poles came to America to Jamestown, where they left their mark as skilled artisans. But the names that come first to mind are those heroes who came not as immigrants but as volunteers in the cause of American liberty. One never returned to his native land. General Casimir Pulaski was mortally wounded at the Battle of Savannah and died on October 11, 1779 onboard the WASP, a ship of the Colonial Navy. The site of his grave is unknown.

The temporal remains of Thaddeus Kosciuszko are entombed in the crypt of St. Leonard in the Cathedral of St. Stanislaw at Wawel Castle in Cracow. In that crypt, on October 17, 1977, the Bicentennial anniversary of the victory at Saratoga in which General Kosciuszko played a key role, prominent Poles and Americans participated in ceremonies in his honor. Kosciuszko's burial place was marked on that historic occasion with a bronze plaque as a gift to the people of Poland by a Joint Resolution of Congress, which I had the privilege of introducing in the House of Representatives. The plaque bears the inscription, both in English and Polish: "A Grateful America

Remembers . . . Fighter For Your and Our Freedom."

The Bishop of Cracow, then Cardinal Wojtyla, attending a convocation in Rome, wrote on this occasion: "Our compatriots, who also as Americans hold dear their Polish heritage, are gathered today to commemorate with a special plaque at Kosciuszko's tomb his contribution to the independence of the United States of America . . . Let this celebration at his sarcophagus enkindle the same love that fired the heart of our hero. Let it encourage us to serve that same immortal cause."

The bonds that were forged between Poland and America more than two centuries ago have grown stronger over time. They have been strengthened in many ways despite Poland's military alliance with the Soviet Union and most other communist nations of Europe in the Warsaw Pact, the Soviet counterpart to NATO.

Increased trade has resulted from Poland's "most favored nation" status; educational, scientific, medical and cultural exchanges have multiplied and people-to-people programs have flourished.

One of the earliest of these is the American Children's Hospital in Cracow, which since its inception has provided medical treatment for over one million Polish children. Built largely from Polish zlotys accruing to the account of the United States from the sale of agricultural surpluses and made available through Congressional initiative, the hospital was dedicated in 1965 as a lasting tribute to the friendship between the American and Polish peoples. Limited aid through grants, under the

American Schools and Hospitals Abroad program has helped fund vital equipment and specialized medical training provided by Project HOPE with the cooperation of American hospitals and their staffs.

The heritage of Poland is rich in religious tradition, and deeply imbued with a love for knowledge and learning in every field of human endeavor as well as of music, literature and art in all its forms. Taken together with a history of being a fiercely independent people, these traits make up the Polish spirit. The music of Frederic Chopin is so uniquely identified with that spirit that the Nazi army of occupation forbade the rendering of his compositions by Poles under the pain of death.

This is a book about the ethnic heritage of three generations of a family which has its origins in Poland and thrives now on two continents. This is a story engagingly told, which is typical of the stories of many immigrants from Poland. It is an account with which millions of Americans can identify and will help countless others to understand our justifiable pride in our Polish heritage and the yearning of the Polish spirit for freedom, man's inevitable destiny.

Clement J. Zablocki,
Chairman, Committee on Foreign
  Affairs
U.S. House of Representatives,
Washington, D.C.

In Walnut Creek, California, and in other places in that state, there are many thousands of walnut trees that strike the visitor as very strange. These trees have a dark bark about a quarter of the way up their slim trunks and a much lighter bark from that point upward. The trees are hybrids. The lower sections are native American walnut which develop strong root systems even in inhospitable soil. The upper parts are English walnut grafted on because of their superior ability to bear nuts. The trees are among the most productive in the world.

GENESIS
OF A
JOURNEY

CHAPTER ONE

PRESIDENT John Fitzgerald Kennedy took the four steps of the hastily-built speaker's platform gingerly. The back, always annoying, was especially tender in the damp Irish spring. A slight stoop, but a bright smile. Handshakes only slightly tentative, then a few quick steps to the microphone. As he spoke, his right hand alternately jabbed the air for emphasis and dipped self-consciously into his suit pocket.

"When my great-grandfather left here to become a cooper in East Boston, he carried nothing with him except a strong faith and desire for liberty. I'm glad to say that all of his great-grandchildren value that inheritance . . . If he hadn't left, I'd be working for the Albatross Company or for John T. Kelly's shop over there!"

The crowd loved it.

It was June, 1963. He was on the tube back in America. And he was saying the things that I and millions of Americans had often thought. "What if Grampa hadn't left the old country? What would I be if he hadn't come? What's it like back there where so many generations of the family lived and died? I've got to see the place. I've got to see the people."

That kind of thinking—that "itch"—started with me long before the Irish American President focused it with his visit to the land of his great-grandfather. You'd know the feeling if you were born and raised in any of the hundreds of ethnic neighborhoods across the country. You'd know just how right the Pan Am commercial was, a few years ago, when it reminded us that "Every American has two heritages."

Two heritages. That's certainly my story. My first school was St. Stanislaus Kostka in Greenpoint, Brooklyn, where we routinely spoke Polish in the classroom. I spent most of my free time with Tadeusz, Edziu and Wladziu. At home, I listened to the grave conversations about the 1939 invasion and quick subjugation of Poland. But on special days, I cavorted at Polish American dances, picnics and weddings. Not that I was illiterate in English or uncaring about things American. I had two languages and, yes, two heritages.

Of course, not all Americans feel quite so warm about an "old country." For those whose ancestors arrived here a few hundred years ago, the "roots" emotions are likely to be shallow. It's somewhat the same for those who are products of many generations of "ethnic mixing." I feel a little sorry for them because they've missed out on something good and warm and even vital.

But the millions of Americans who have preserved an

identity with an old country or culture—without diluting their appreciation of this country—well, they know what I was feeling when I resolved that some day I'd see Poland and the villages of my forebears.

It wasn't until 1979 that I surrendered to that "itch."

This is the story of my visit to Poland in the summer of 1979. I made the trip with the perfect guide, my 71-year-old father who had left there in 1927—52 years earlier—and had never returned. We walked the narrow streets of the village where, as far as we could determine, the Paluszek family originated; and we strolled the broad boulevards of Poland's ancient cities. I saw and felt more than I could have hoped for. He saw much that he remembered and much that simply hadn't existed when he was last there.

There is a second level to my American Journey. It is the three-generation journey of my family in America. Starting with grandfather Jozef who left Poland in 1903, we've come a long way in those three generations. Our 1979 visit to Poland was a culmination, a celebration, of *this* journey, this family experience spread over seventy-six years.

More than likely, this is a story not unlike your own family's. Because all of us *are* from somewhere else. And for many of us, "somewhere else" just won't fade away.

IN MANY WAYS it was fitting that my father and I visited Poland a few months after one of the most celebrated pilgrimmages of the century, the visit of Pope John Paul II. Because one of his many engaging remarks during his visit to Poland helped spark the trip. On the outskirts of Crakow, within sight of the rugged Tatra Mountains, he told several hundred thousand people that the region's infertile soil had caused many farmers from the area to migrate, mostly to America. "I hope," said the Pope, "that when they became Americans, they still remain highlanders all the same."

We came from a section of Poland not far from the Tatras. "Highlanders" in America? Yes, because even after two generations there existed a sweet ache to experience the old country. Some psychologists say it is the inevitable reaction to uprooting, an emotion bordering on the Hebraic.

The "itch" had been building all through the year. It had also been fed by Vice President Walter Mondale's visit to Mundal, Norway, the town his great-grandfather left in 1856.

The Vice President, greeted by virtually the entire population (400) of the picturesque village nestled beneath an awesome glacier, responded, "I don't know many of you, but all of your faces are familiar." Paying tribute to his forebears who migrated to America, Mondale touched the tap root: "What a challenge that must have been. Leaving their friends, their home, their church, their farm, everything they knew to go to America, to a new land they knew little about. What brave people they must have been! I wonder how many members of my generation would have as much courage as they did."

I couldn't help thinking about Grandfather Jozef. I

6

had to know more about him. Why did he come here? How hard was it for him in Poland? And how hard was it here?

Fortunately, dad and his sister Sophie, (who had come from Poland for a short visit,) gave me some vital insights.

CHAPTER TWO

JOZEF (1885–1969)

THERE WAS nothing idealistic about it.

Orphaned at twelve, he was eighteen years old with little education and, more important, no prospect of owning land in a country where land meant everything. Poland in 1903 just couldn't support the likes of Jozef Paluszek. It was time to look elsewhere.

The big landlords dominated the area around the village of Lipnica, about seventy miles east of Cracow, in the southeastern part of Poland. Counts and barons descended from a Polish gentry now only a dim memory still owned most of the desirable farmland and forests. On the poorer land, small farms had multiplied as inheritances split modest-sized properties into acreages that could barely support small farm families. But Jozef wasn't going to inherit even that kind of marginal land.

The joys of childhood had passed quickly. A little fishing and hunting and games with friends, but mostly work on neighboring farms. Of course, there had been school, for a while, anyway. A school where teachers knew that their pupils would get no more than an elementary education, if that. A school where only the basics counted. Reading, writing, sums and—as important as any of these practical skills—religion and the history of Poland.

WHAT WAS THIS "POLAND," anyway?

As a nation it didn't exist. In fact, it hadn't existed for about a hundred years. How could Jozef think of himself as "Polish?" He lived in Austria Hungary, as had his parents and grandparents. How could Poland, a "nation" without a state, exist?

Poland existed only in the mind. Millions of people kept it alive and identified with it. In regions like Jozef's Galicia, under Austrian control, as well as in German- and Russian-occupied lands, somehow the *idea* of Poland survived. Incredibly, it would survive a hundred and twenty-three years of such partition and would be born again only in the "new order" established after World War I. This idea, however—this concept of Poland— had for all of the years of partition a life force like that of a healthy plant needing to break through the earth's surface despite all obstacles.

Jozef had learned Polish history well. The Catholic church, and the national public education system (established in 18th-century pre-partition Poland) delivered training in the Polish culture and history to school children in all three occupation zones. The Catholic clergy, who were given free access to the public schools for religious instruction, always seemed to work Polish history into the religion lessons.

9

It began with the great medieval King Mieszko who built a strong base for the Kingdom of Poland in 966 when he converted to Christianity and married the Slav Princess Dubravka.

Jozef learned that after Mieszko, Polish history was an unending series of bloody battles which moved boundaries forward and back in regions like Pomerania on the Baltic, Silesia in the west, Lithuania in the north and the Ukraine in the east.

He quivered at the story of the murder of the Bishop of Cracow, Stanislaus, by King Boleslas the Bold in 1079. He gloried in the pivotal battle of Lignica in 1241 where "the advances of the Mongol hordes" were halted by Polish forces. He took pride, too, in reading about the founding of the University of Cracow, only the second in Central Europe, by Casimir the Great in 1364.

Then there were the triumphs of triumphs: The epic victory at Grunwald over the Teutonic Order in 1410 and King Jan Sobieski's successful leadership of European forces in the historic Battle of Vienna in 1683, where the advance of Islamic forces into Central Europe was halted forever. On the other hand, there was the tragic series of partitions resisted unsuccessfully by patriots like Thaddeusz Kosciuszko (returned from helping America throw off the British yoke). Then came the partition agreement in 1795 by Russia, Prussia and Austria "to abolish Poland forever." Somehow it generated a spirit among the Polish people that would be longlived—a spirit articulated by the anthem written about the same time as the French Marsellaise. It began with a pledge:

10

"Poland is still living
While we are alive."

Of course, as part of his Polish history lessons, young Jozef and his friends were also introduced to some less significant, if not less colorful, figures—Boleslaus Krzywousty (the wry-mouthed), Wladyslaw Laskonogi (spindleshanks) and Wladyslaw Łokietek (the short).

EQUALLY IMPORTANT, Jozef learned that over the centuries, Poland had established an identity that would abide even until his own day (and, although he couldn't know it, even to the era of his great-grandchildren): Political and spiritual alliance with the Roman Catholic Church; a "grand concept of Europe," conceived way back when duchies, fiefdoms and tribes were generally the ultimate in Central European political sophistication; the concept of Poland as buffer between East and West, often with tragic consequences; and the importance of literature, art and music in the development of a nation and an individual.

Jozef and other young Poles learned of their country's rich tradition of republicanism and democracy. They were taught that in 1189 (25 years before the Magna Carta), the Kingdom of Poland guaranteed its citizens equal protection under the law, and that as early as 1343 King Casimir the Great introduced the principle of habeas corpus in the country.

ALL THAT WAS GRAND, but by the time he was eighteen, Jozef had decided that even rich tradition didn't offset the obstacles to a happy and successful life then and there. He had been a servant for the neighboring landlord. He had done odd jobs in the village. And he had developed a reputation as an ambitious, gregarious young man who wanted much more out of life than being a farmhand. Some folks thought him uppity, bragging about his brothers Mike and Nick in America. Mike, he was sure, would give him a chance to break out of his rut. And after a few years in America, Jozef would send for the youngest of the Paluszek brothers, Martin. Till then, Martin would be alright with relatives nearby.

Why America? After all, Austria-occupied Poland had a growing industrial base. There were a few steel mills and wood-products companies and breweries. Cotton, raised in the Lipnica area, was processed nearby. And light industry was beginning to bloom in Rzeszow, only thirty miles away. But, he'd tell his friends, "Mike writes to me about America, about Pennsylvania and Connecticut. Do you know what the farms are like in Pennsylvania and Connecticut? And you don't have to inherit one. You can save enough money in a few years to buy one. Or if you want to work in the city, there are all kinds of jobs.

"You know how many Polish people there are in America? Almost as many as here!"

The arrangements made, Jozef left Lipnica in the spring of 1903. Enroute to his trans-Atlantic passage, he travelled not to Warsaw and the Baltic, but through Germany and France. Travel through Russian-occupied Poland presented all kinds of obstacles for young and

12

healthy Polish males who were subject to 30 years of service in the Russian Army. He boarded one of the many trans-Atlantic steamers at Le Havre, spent twelve days in steerage, and arrived here as one of 857,046 immigrants to be admitted to America in the twelve months ending June 30th, 1903. It was a record year for American immigration. As a matter of fact, more than 12 million immigrants would pass through the New York City "Isle of Tears"—Ellis Island—from 1892 to 1924 in what was part of the largest voluntary migration in the world history.

I can imagine how Jozef handled the "Isle of Tears."

Short, stocky, healthy and ambitious, he was confident throughout the examination. No potential ward of the state here. Ready to join Mike or take any promising job right here in the city he had seen only from the ship's deck. Joking, chatting, making new friends. A young man with a new life beginning to spread before him.

Despite the heavy human traffic at Ellis Island—as many as 12,000 people a day—it was all over in three hours. He was on the ferry to New York City where Mike would meet him. The babel of his fellow immigrants mixed with the English spoken by ferry sailors. The city skyline, modest by today's standards, was nevertheless imposing to this farm laborer who had never seen a building taller than the cathedral in Rzeszow. He wasn't fazed at all. He drank it all in. He could move and grow in this kind of country.

Mike met him at the ferry landing in Brooklyn and they stayed with some relatives overnight in the Northside section of Williamsburg, just across the East River from midtown. But there would be no tarrying. Mike was a miner and had to be back at work with little delay. The next morning they ferried across both the East River and the Hudson and boarded the Erie and Lackawana Railroad near Weehawken. Five hours later they were at the depot in Wilkes Barre.

WILKES BARRE was better than Lipnica, but somehow not all that America could be. Mining coal, which Jozef tried for three weeks, was just not his idea of the best America had to offer. A few months after arrival, Jozef decided to take his chances in New York City. "I'm going all the way with this little adventure," he thought. "There's no turning back to Poland. Farming is more promising here, but it's not as promising as a lot of other things."

Going all the way meant, first, getting a hold on the new language. Jozef could see how a bilingual ability could lead to supervisory positions, the buffer jobs between management and workers who spoke only Polish.

Three months later, he was living in a boarding house in Northside and commuting on the Kent Avenue trolley to work as a machinist's helper at the American Manufacturing Company's jute mill on Franklin Street in neighboring Greenpoint. Both the residence and the job were the results of an "old-boy" network that had developed among the Polish immigrants. The arrivals from Austria-controlled Poland tended to congregate in

14

the Northside area, whereas those from German- and Russian-occupied Poland lived mainly in Greenpoint. But the two communities were joined by the Polish-oriented Roman Catholic Church, St. Stanislaus Kostka, on Driggs Avenue in Greenpoint. St. Stanislaus was building a handsome new church.

One of Jozef's roommates, a native of a town not far from Lipnica, had been working at the jute mill for a year when Jozef came to Northside. "For someone like you, especially if you pick up English as fast as you plan to, the job should be a cinch." Jozef applied and got the entry-level job with no difficulty.

Nine months later, in early 1904, he completed his first night-school course in English. Not long afterward, his surprising mechanical aptitude helped him earn a promotion to stationery engineer. Later he rose to superintendent. During his ten years at the jute mill, he was so highly regarded that top management offered him a chance to become the assistant general manager of its plant in India. "No thanks," said Jozef, "America, not India, is where I want to spend my life." Later he would move to a still higher paying production job at the Jack Frost sugar refinery in Long Island City, Queens.

MARY KONEFAL was sixteen years old when she left Lipnica where her family had farmed for about a hundred years. She had decided to follow in the footsteps of her three older brothers who had come to America just before the turn of the century. Northside would be Mary's home and while she studied English at

15

night school she'd work in the jute mill. She preferred that to the only other job available, that of a domestic in nearby middle-class Brooklyn homes.

A pretty girl with long dark hair and green eyes, she was popular in the fast growing Polish community of young immigrants in Northside. There were periods of loneliness, of course, and an occasional painful longing for the farm in Lipnica. But the farm would have to be just a memory. As the fourth of six children, there was no way she would inherit it. So she, like many of her friends, set about making a life in America.

Where they met—at a dance, a wedding, at night school or at the jute mill—isn't important. The fact is that, born and raised within a few miles of each other in Poland, Jozef and Mary met in Brooklyn. It was not all that usual among immigrants. Some of the neighborhood elders advised patience, a little better foundation in America before marriage. But they were married in January, 1907 at St. Stanislaus. He was twenty-two, she was eighteen.

They would live in a series of cold water flats in Northside as the family grew. And it grew quickly; a first son, John was born in January, 1908.

A year later, their world was turned upside down.

The letter arrived, of course, while Jozef was at work. When he got home, Mary was beside herself. "They're giving me the farm! My father says that his sons aren't coming back from America and that he wants us to take over the farm. Of course, they'll stay on, we'll have to take care of them, but the farm will be ours."

Choice land in Poland. Total independence. A chance to break through at home. Weigh that against the long range possibility of an as-yet-unfocused potential success in America. Characteristically, Jozef chose both.

His plan was simple. He'd accept the Konefals' offer of the farm, but as long as they were well enough to run it, he would stay in America, saving money to improve and expand the farm. Mary could visit there from time to time to make sure that all was well and that her parents were up to working the farm.

Jozef, after all, was growing not only in his career but in the Polish American community. Shortly after arriving here, he had joined the local chapter of a Chicago-headquartered Polish National Alliance. This group, like similar organizations serving other immigrant communities, was sort of a combination lodge and insurance cooperative. It wasn't that Polish Americans or other ethnics couldn't get life insurance from the big American insurance companies. It was just that they felt much more comfortable dealing with "their own kind." Several similar Polish American organizations had found great favor among the recent immigrants. Jozef was soon a leader of the Northside chapter and used many of the meetings to refine his now impressive speaking abilities. Among other special benefits, the chapter established a fund for sick leave for its members. Jozef was a trustee.

These organizations were part of "Polonia," the Polish American community that was a tightly-drawn circle for the preservation of what the first-generation immigrants held dear.

DESPITE THE TERRIBLE DEVASTATION of World War I, by 1918 Jozef and Mary were well along in their plan to develop the farm. Late in 1909, Mary had brought her young son John to Lipnica. He had remained there when she returned to America in 1913. Seven years later, she returned to Poland, this time bringing four more sons (Joseph, Anthony, Raymond and Adam) born in America. She also brought money to improve the farm. Then, in 1922 she returned to America once again.

Finally, in 1925 Jozef and Mary agreed that it was time to go home. They had accumulated all they were likely to. The sprawling family now included a sixth child, their first daughter, Mary. The Konefals were aging. It was time to settle down in Poland. In the summer of 1925, Jozef saw Lipnica again for the first time in twenty-two years.

In Poland, a seventh child, Sophie, would be born in 1927, and an eighth, Jacob, in 1930.

There was no way to know, in 1925, that within the next two decades World War II would leave Poland demolished and defenseless; that its cities and farms would be ravaged by armies moving back and forth over this "buffer" for almost five years; that an occupation more brutal and oppressive than that of the Partition would have to be endured.

Jozef and his family were not exactly welcomed by the neighbors at Lipnica. Not unlike the situation that "New Yorkicans" would face when they returned to Puerto Rico in the 1960s' and 1970s', it was difficult, indeed, to "go home again." There was the relative affluence of the returnees. More important, their attitude was downright foreign. Jozef caused raised eyebrows in the village square soon after he returned from America when he refused to offer the customary obeisances—a bow and kiss of the hand—to the local nobleman-landlord. "Who does he think he is?" the villagers would mumble. "He goes to America, comes back here with a few dollars and thinks he can set himself above the rest of us. He'd better get used to the idea that he's not in America anymore."

So Jozef and Mary, with their brood of eight children (the eldest, John, would leave for America in May, 1927 as if to complete the cycle his father had begun in 1903) began to look for a new farm. In early 1927, they sold the farm in Lipnica, added their American-generated savings to the proceeds, and bought a larger farm with more fertile soil fifteen miles away. The new place, in Kolbuszowa, was small by American standards—a little more than fifty acres. But with its brick farmhouse, newer equipment and nearness to a sizable village market, it was all they could ever want.

BY EARLY 1939, THE WAR was obviously inevitable. Still, when it came, it struck with a fury few Poles could have anticipated. The Polish high command had built an army based primarily on cavalry. The defense strategy depended on quick mobilization by Poland's allies, Great Britain and France. When the German blitzkrieg hit and Britain and France moved only in defense of their own strategic positions, the Polish cause was lost. The Russian "stab in the back," a surprise alliance with Hitler and invasion from the east, was the crushing blow.

It was over in a month. But not before much slaughter. The German light artillery, tanks and well-equipped infantry clashed with the Polish cavalry at Kolbuszowa with predictable results. Much of the town was reduced to rubble. A small mountain of dead horses lay rotting in the village square. The occupation began.

Even for Nazi Germany, the efficiency was impressive.

First there was the inventory. Every farm animal, every piece of equipment, in fact anything of value was registered. And everything was to have only one use— support of the German war effort. Every Pole, natural slaves in Third Reich social philosophy, would have to work to support that effort. Some, like Jozef, could fulfill that obligation where they were, producing as much food as possible for the New Order. For others, the new obligation was heavier; almost every family in the village had one or more member "exported" to Germany or other occupied industrial centers to work in factories producing weapons or munitions. Many never returned.

Jozef and the Gestapo didn't get along. He was just obstinate enough to resist some of their decrees. That obstinacy almost cost him his life. Violating a strict prohibition, he decided to grow a calf for family consumption "right under the noses of the Niemcy." In a surprise search, the Gestapo found the calf and took Jozef to Rzeszow to await charges on what was a capital offense. Fortunately, a boarder at the Paluszek farm was well connected at Gestapo headquarters. A gallon of honey and ten pounds of butter were bartered for Jozef's release.

In another defiant episode, he succeeded. He had hidden a quart of whiskey in a grain barrel when the Gestapo arrived accompanied by a reluctant Kolbuszowa policeman. It was the policeman who spotted the whiskey. He pushed it further down in the barrel, and on the way out whispered to Jozef, "I'll be back for a taste in a little while."

Other capital offenses included sheltering Jews (and several villagers paid the price for that) and, of course, support of the underground. The scene in wartime American movies where one in ten villagers are chosen to be shot in retribution for acts of the underground is not fiction. Jozef witnessed it more than once in Kolbus-zowa. However, the Nazi's organized murder of millions fell heavier in the larger cities.

LIBERATION came in July, 1944. It arrived with Russian tanks and infantry and was greeted with restrained enthusiasm. "We've traded one devil for another," was the way most of Jozef's friends felt. Still, it was a relief. The front had been stalled just east of Kolbuszowa all through the previous winter. And the Polish First Army, re-constituted by the Allies, was nearby.

But in 1944, the Russian presence on Polish soil, as so many times in earlier centuries, was a source of anxiety.

In contrast with the efficiency of the German oppression, the Russians were totally unpredictable. They were given to spontaneous "adventures" and then periods of relative calm. Russian soldiers seemed to have a compulsion to own wristwatches. The local joke was "A Russian will give you two good horses for a beat-up wristwatch. Then he'll come back late at night and steal back the horses."

Jozef and his family had their share of close shaves with the Russian temperament. One night in early 1945, a dozen Russian enlisted men had had a snoot-full and were getting ugly as they ambled down the road to the Paluszek farmhouse. They banged on the front door, shouted obscenities and were on the verge of looting and worse. All of a sudden, three Russian officers stepped out of the main bedroom. Jozef's farmhouse had been used to billet several officers and he had woke them as the boisterous soldiers approached. The incident was over in a moment.

The coming of the socialist order was another occasion for the "positivism" ("let's see how we can live with it") developed by Poles during the Partition. The good news was land reform. The bad news was the price paid for it.

Polish landlords were exiled to Siberia, their lands distributed broadly, often to totally inexperienced villagers. This, and the experiment in state ownership of much of the land (which drove many experienced small farmers off their land and into factory work in the cities), would prove to be a disaster for farm efficiency. Jobs in the village went first to the "poor." Jozef and his family found themselves somewhere in between the exiled land barons and "the poor." Sophie, the surviving Paluszek daughter (her elder sister, Mary, died during the war) had difficulty getting a job because her father was "rich." Harranguing local Communist bureaucrats, she'd shout, "Look, we have nothing—absolutely nothing—in the house. If we're 'rich', what do you call 'poor' in Russia?" Eventually she got a job in a Kolbuszowa factory and later in the Import-Export Bureau.

JOZEF CAME BACK to America one more time. It was May, 1958. The Polish Socialist government had eased up on travel restrictions. He wanted to see the five sons who had emigrated, to see how they were doing in New York, Michigan and Arizona, and to see his nine American grandchildren.

I saw him for the first time from an observation deck as he inched his was through the customs check at Idlewild (later John F. Kennedy) Airport in New York. The entry took about thirty minutes. America had certainly progressed since his arrival fifty-five years earlier at Ellis Island.

It was very late at night. His flight from Montreal, where he had debarked from the Polish liner Batory had been delayed several hours. Three of his sons were there with their wives and assorted grandchildren. He was short, round, heavy and a bit bent. He came through the door into a small sea of arms and damp eyes. He was caught up in the group and the individual identities

23

didn't become clear for a few minutes. Slowly, everyone fell into place—even his two great-grandsons, one a toddler and the other an infant.

I spent as much time as I could with him during his brief stay in New York. We rode the subway from Queens into Manhattan and at one stop his still-sharp eyes lit up as he announced, "Boro Hall, Brooklyn. That's where I got my marriage license about fifty years ago."

We arrived in the heart of the city. As we walked slowly up the stairs and into the daylight at Rockefeller Plaza, he began what seemed to me to be a giggle. He seemed to be intoxicated by the tall buildings, by the bustle, by the fantastic change in New York in thirty three years. But before long, he was back in his element. As we walked slowly down Fifth Avenue, he looked east and west on one of the broader streets and said, "I like that 57th Street. That's a good street." As if he was ready to buy it.

He went home. But we have the pictures. In one he sits with his great-grandsons; together they span four generations of the American experience, the American Journey.

Mary died of a heart attack in 1968. Jozef, 84, died of a stroke a year later. His remaining children in Poland, Sophie and Jacob, shared the farm in Kolbuszowa. Neither share is adequate as a working farm. Jozef's legacy lies not in Poland but in America.

Still, I had to see where he came from and where he returned. I had to see Poland.

CHAPTER THREE

While preparing for the trip to Poland, I asked my father to tell me about his life there and his life here in America. We sat and talked into a tape recorder for hours. Here's what he said:

JOHN (1909–)

I DON'T RECALL my mother taking me to Poland. I was only two years old. But as far back as I can remember, I had it in the back of my mind to return to America. It wasn't just that my parents, and later my brothers, were here. That was tough, but my grandparents were wonderful to me. In some ways they were better than parents because they felt they had to make up for my parents being away. But I was an American, so I knew someday I'd go back.

Anyway, what was life like in Poland? It was very hard. Farm life then was almost all handwork and even when you were only five or six there was plenty for you to do.

Then there was the war. I'll never forget how we heard

that war was declared. In those days, the village had sort of a town crier who used to make important announcements. Only this fellow had a bugle and people would gather round because they knew something important was happening.

Well, this day in 1914—I remember it was hot, so it must have been summer, maybe late August—my grandfather and I were in the village and we heard him announce that Russia was at war with Austria and Germany. My grandfather said to a friend, "We know what that means, don't we? Poland will be their battlefield." He was right. Before the winter began, the shooting was within a few miles of our village.

The artillery was scary. We built bunkers just outside the house. The bunkers were about 15 feet square, covered with heavy timbers. They weren't beautiful, but let me tell you, when you heard the shells passing overhead, you were glad to be down there.

The soldiers were with us all the time. From the time I was six years old they were with us. And it was tough. I don't mean that they were brutal. They were just soldiers—often hungry and tired and sometimes scared. Naturally, they took whatever they wanted from the farm. What little was left was ours.

I remember having to go to the barn when my grandmother milked the cows so I could get a drink of milk before it got to the house where the soldiers would drink it fast. And I remember Grandma hiding a loaf of bread she baked so we could share it late at night.

The soldiers weren't bad to us. If they had enough, they would share their food. But if they were hard up, they'd take what they could from us. Like soldiers anywhere, I guess.

One time my friend and I saw a company of soldiers

cooking a big piece of beef around a campfire. We went over to them and hung around with the biggest eyes we could make. When a soldier gave us each a chunk, we took off like bullets. We took the meat home to save it and were back at the campfire five minutes later. Big eyes didn't work this time. "You couldn't have eaten that meat so fast" our soldier friend yelled, starting to get up. "Get out of here before I kick you to Rzeszow." We ran.

Propaganda? The first time the Russians were coming, we thought the world was going to end. We had been told stories how they liked to chop off ears and breasts and gouge eyes just for sport. We were all running into the forest when my grandfather remembered that he left something in the farm-house, so he went back. Before he got there, he was intercepted by a Russian patrol which asked him a couple of questions and let him return. When he reached us, no one would believe that he saw the Russians. "Old man, if you saw the Russki," one neighbor said, "you wouldn't have all your equipment."

The Russians overran our farm in late 1914. I remember the first day there, they ate about 50 chickens. When they moved on, we had only two left. A few months later, the Austrian army was back, only to be pushed back by the Russians a few months after that. We felt like the rope in a tug-of-war. Then, one more time, the Austrians pushed the Russians out and all the way back to where they came from. It was late 1915 and the Russian army was crumbling.

You know, it's strange about war. Before a war—or even after a war—it seems so big. But when you're living through one, when armies are coming and going and coming again, when you start to see things over and over again—even if they're horrible—you get numb. I was only six, seven, eight years old, and I was getting numb. Hardly anything bothered me.

We began to hear about a Pole, Jozef Pilsudski. My grandfather said that maybe out of all this turmoil, someone like Pilsudski might be able to end the Partition. That was unbelievable but we wanted so much to believe it. A hundred and twenty years of Partition. No Poland in all that time. And some Poles were even fighting against each other in this crazy war. Those in the Russian zone of occupation were drafted into that army. Others in Austria and Germany were under arms with those countries. And still others went to France to fight against Germany.

But Pilsudski was a real hero to us. Before the war, he was an underground leader fighting the Tsarist government in a secret organization called the Union of Active Struggle. In 1915, he was leading a special detachment in the Austrian army called the Polish Legion. "He's a man to watch," my grandfather said.

FOR US on the Eastern Front, the war was all but over in 1916. Russia was collapsing. The Central Powers, which thought they could win us over by declaring that there was now a Kingdom of Poland under their protection, now had their hands full on the Western Front.

I started school about then, when I was seven and a half or eight. I remember I had to walk about two miles to the school, the same one in Lipnica that my father had gone to. When I got there, a school wall had shell holes in it. But they somehow patched it pretty quickly and we didn't think any more about the holes. We had two shifts at that school. If you had to work on the farm in the morning, you went to school in the afternoon and vice versa. There were four grades. I was with the youngest grade in 1916. The oldest kids in school were about thirteen, maybe fourteen. After that, you were expected to work on the farm fulltime.

We had some good teachers. I remember Mr. and Mrs. Piecara teaching me in the upper grades. They really cared about their young farmer students.

But you didn't get promoted one grade to the next unless you passed all the tests. They didn't care if you stayed in one grade forever, you didn't move up unless you proved you were ready. Of course, some kids who were "slow" would drop out. My grandparents were like all the other farmers in the area; they wanted me to know how to read and write and some geography and history, but there was not much talk about "higher education." I don't blame them. That's the way it was there.

The school vacation was strictly timed with the harvest, in the summer. It had to be. Most of the parents would have kept the children home to help with the harvest anyway. I finished what we'd call here grammar school—eighth grade—and that was it.

Our farm raised potatoes, cabbage, lettuce, barley, wheat, oats and rye, all at the same time on this little place, maybe fifty acres. Our farms were very narrow because they had been split many times over a lot of generations. Ours was less than a hundred feet wide and maybe two miles long with several different types of soil on it. When I came to America and saw pictures of the big wheat fields here in the midwest, I couldn't believe it.

Harvest time was beautiful. You ever see those western

movies where all the farmers come to one farm with their horses and wagons to harvest the crops, and then move on to the next farm? That's the way it was. Everybody cooperated.

THE LOCAL CATHOLIC CHURCH was an important part of all of our lives. Everybody went to church every Sunday, no exceptions unless you were dying. We had to walk four miles each way and just about everyone did it. The only questioning I heard was from some young people who came back to the village after being uprooted during the fighting. That didn't last too long. But sometimes we'd be walking and our "neighbor," the big landlord, would pass us in his horse and carriage. The landlords had special pews in the church and we couldn't sit in them.

I just remembered something else: In Poland, the parish always owned some farmland and had a few farmworkers; I never saw that here in America, but then again there wasn't much farmland in Brooklyn.

The Catholic church was so strong that each parish in the Austrian zone was partly supported by tax revenues.

There were a lot of devotions and pilgrimages to Czestochowa and other shrines. I can still remember my grandmother *singing* the rosary at home.

There were no "Catholic schools." We didn't need them. The population was so heavily Catholic that the priest came to our public school to give us instruction. I never heard of a "Catholic school" until I came to this country.

First Communion was really a big occasion. You had to take instructions for two or three years, and then you had to go one-on-one with the priest in a special room in the schoolhouse. But when you passed, and a group was ready, it was a big event in the village—everybody wore their best clothes and there was a big ceremony with lots of wild flowers on the altar and all the proud parents and relatives. The church where I made my first communion has to be about 150 years old. I hope it's still standing. I'd love to see it.

There were a few non-Catholics in our area, a few Jewish storekeepers in the village and a small Lutheran community about eight miles away. We all got along.

Sickness and death? We handled them like peasants anywhere in the world. Our nearest doctor was about fifteen miles away, so we didn't see him unless it was pretty serious. No telephone. No electricity. The nearest hospital was in Rzeszow about thirty miles away. But we had home remedies for colds and other minor problems. Did they work? Who knows? We *thought* they worked, and sometimes that's enough.

We didn't have any central heating, only the big fireplace in one of the two rooms we had in the house. We didn't have indoor plumbing. And the winters could be rough. I remember snow on the ground from December to March. But somehow it seems to me people get more colds over here.

WERE THE PEOPLE HAPPY? There wasn't much choice. You had to be satisfied with your lot. You knew exactly what was in store for you, just how far you could go in life. There was not much complaining. People accepted their lot, the way their parents and grandparents and earlier generations had accepted.

But people had, what do you call it, "outlets." Like weddings. A lot of them really *did* last for two or three days. They started with a celebration the day *before*. The houses of the village were decorated. The women made special traditional clothing. No rent-a-tuxedo. And the food! Special meat

31

dishes and fancy breads and cakes and plenty to drink. Dancing and singing late into the night and then starting again the next day. Then too, christenings, confirmations, first communions—they were all reasons to have big parties. There, it was all done by the relatives and friends, no caterers.

If crime is a sign of unhappiness, we were a very happy people. There was very little robbery or any other serious crime. We had two policemen to cover an area about ten square miles.

We didn't have any sports. But there was a little pond a mile away and we would go swimming once in a while. I had a good friend, Frank Dól, who was in the same boat—born in America and being raised by grandparents on a nearby farm. On hot days, we would hit that swimming hole as soon as we finished our chores.

But as I got a little older, I started to notice a few things. For instance, the big landlords were very arrogant. You could never mix with them in the village. And all the people who worked for them used to step aside and bow when the landlords' carriages came through town.

It was sickening. I guess that's when I started to think seriously about coming to America, because it looked to me like it was always going to be like that in Poland.

Of course, just about all the marriages were matches by the parents. A young man who was going to inherit a farm was a good catch; his parents could demand quite a dowry from the parents of the "matched" young woman.

THE MOST EXCITING DAY I spent in Poland was our first Constitution Day in May, 1919—the day a resurrected Poland celebrated its freedom and its great historic document.

Imagine! Cut up into pieces for over a hundred years and

suddenly the country was whole and alive again. "All the people since 1795 who worked and prayed for this," one of the neighbors said as we watched the celebration. "And we're the lucky ones."

What a celebration!

Parades, bands, beautiful horses pulling specially decorated wagons, lots of food and drink—it was like the best Fourth of July they ever had here.

And you know what? My grandfather was right about Pilsudski. He was one of the leaders who set up a new Polish government in November, 1918. Then in the next few years, his Polish Legions got so strong they formed the main part of a new Polish army that pushed the Russian Communist Army all the way from Warsaw well back into their own country. Think of that! After over a hundred twenty years of Partition by Russia and other countries, *we had an army in Russia!* Sure, the Russians were weak because of their revolution, but to Poles that didn't matter. What mattered was that the chains were off—completely off. At one point in 1920, the Polish army captured Kiev. Then the armies went back and forth, before the Treaty of Riga ceded territories in the Ukraine and Byelorussia to Poland.

"GYPSIES, it must be a small bunch of gypsies," I figured. It was May of 1920 and I was taking our four cows to pasture. I could see this small group of people about a half mile down the road. It was a rag-tag bunch with maybe a dozen children running alongside a wagon.

When they got to the entrance of our farm, a woman and four little boys left the group and started down the road. All of a sudden the four boys came running and screaming at the cows. The animals took off across the meadow and didn't stop until they were a half mile away. I was livid. "John, stop screaming at those boys, they're your brothers," said my mother, home from Brooklyn with Joseph, Anthony, Raymond, and Adam, ages 6 to 2. The cows took a long time to get used to these kids from Brooklyn.

For the next seven years, I was big brother to these guys, gradually breaking them into the farm routine. Was the house crowded? By your standards yes, by ours then, well, who knew any better? Tony slept with me and the three other boys slept in another bed. Somehow there was room for five boys and three adults in two big rooms. There was plenty of fresh vegetables and milk, but very few "treats." I think that's why all of us had such good teeth. American dentists can't believe my teeth.

Meat? Well, that was a different story. We had a meat meal maybe once every two weeks, mostly chicken or pork.

My brothers started school on time and went right through eighth grade without interruption. They were kind of wild from the beginning; after all they had all kinds of room to run in, new "toys" (the animals), and they were "liberated" from my father who was a tough man. My mother was easy-going.

I eventually got over the feeling of being an outsider in my own home. They had come as a group when I was twelve years old. Don't forget that until then I hardly knew my mother. Well, she left again for America in 1922 and the boys and I grew closer. Then I had to be like a father for them—buy clothing and shoes, send them to school. Because my grandparents were getting older.

I had started to think about going to America even before my mother brought the boys to Poland. I always felt that I was an American. After all, I was born here.

34

I had overheard my mother and had listened to some neighbors and cousins talk about this country. "Freedom, jobs and good food for everyone. You can make something of yourself there," they would say.

Well, when my mother and father both came back to Poland to stay, in 1925, I started to make plans. Even before they came back, I used to think about Poland and ask myself, "Is this all there is to life? There has to be more." And there were so many people from our area going to America! Some would stay, but a lot would come back and talk about it. When you'd hear what they had to say and compare it to what you could expect in Poland—an arranged marriage, maybe even more splitting up of the farm, all that stuff—well, it wasn't hard for an *American* to decide.

WHEN I WAS LEAVING—I'll never forget the date, it was Constitution Day, May 3, 1927—and I was eighteen years old—that's the first time my father treated me like a grownup. We had to take the long train ride to Warsaw, about eight hours, and I guess he finally realized that I was going to do it, go off on my own to America. But he wasn't sad about my going. A lot of Polish parents in those days expected that many of their children would leave for America. Anyway, I was glad to talk during the trip because it helped me forget about leaving my grandparents, who I had come to love so much. When I was leaving the farm, grandfather Konefal said to me, "Why do you have to do this? You won't like it there. It's different. It's mixed up. There are all kinds of people. And we're going to miss you so!"

As much as I loved him there was no way he could change my mind. I kissed him and my grandmother and turned away quickly because there were tears on all of our cheeks. We all

35

knew it was goodbye forever. They were in their seventies.

When my father and I got to Warsaw, we had to stay overnight. The next day I got my first good look at a big city. I'll never forget the big park, I think they call it Ogród Saski, near the Tomb of the Unknown Soldier. And the broad avenues. And the old palaces. For a farm boy it was really something. I just gawked all day long.

We had to visit a government office to make sure that my passport and everything else was in order. I'll never forget that. Because a stuffy military man, I think a major, gave me a grilling and for a few minutes I thought somehow they wouldn't let me go. He asked me how was it I wanted to go to America and not serve in the Polish Army. I said, "Because I'm an American. I was born there."

He puffed a bit and said, "Officially, there's nothing I can do but let you go to America, but unofficially let me ask you something. You're a farmer. Suppose you had a cow that wandered over to your neighbor's farm and dropped it's calf there. Whose calf would it be?" I wasn't going to argue with him, so I just shrugged. He signed the necessary papers and I was out the door in a flash.

I said goodbye to my father, boarded a train to Gdynia, which was then just beginning to blossom as the Polish seaport on the Baltic. On May 6th, with one suitcase, I sailed from Gdynia for Le Havre, France. On that little ship, I met a lot of young Polish people who were going to the United States. And there was a man from Lipnica, Joe Venglash, who had made the trip a few times. He and I bunked together. After a couple of days of rough Baltic seas, we passed through the Kiel Canal and the English Channel and arrived at Le Havre.

To a Polish farm boy, Le Havre looked fantastic. I was

used to flat land. But here was a city on two levels—half of it right at the water, and the other half up on a cliff. We had a couple of days in Le Havre, and we walked around, but I didn't have much money, so I didn't buy anything. The food was okay, but the people didn't seem too friendly. Maybe they didn't like the way we talked.

I BROUGHT $20 TO AMERICA. Of course, my passage had been paid for. My bachelor uncle in Pennsylvania, Mike, had advanced the money, about $180, on the condition that I pay it back, with $20 interest, in one year. When the year was up, he really wanted the money. I had almost all of it, but he wouldn't wait. So I borrowed a few dollars and paid him off. I heard that he took the money and gambled it away the next day. Nice guy.

But I'm getting ahead of myself. Let me tell you about coming over on the Isle de France. Joe and I had a small room below deck, maybe ten by twelve feet. He was the experienced traveller, so I tried to listen to what he had to say. He told me not to eat too much because I'd get seasick. Well, I was about a hundred and five pounds, had lived mostly on potatoes and cabbage almost all my life, and all of a sudden I'm surrounded by all kinds of great French food. I figured, hell, I'll take a chance. So I gorged myself for six days and tasted plenty of wine too. And Joe took it easy on the food. But just about every night, I'd bounce into our little room, satisfied and ready for bed, and Joe was in the bathroom —seasick.

We got to New York harbor and I remember thinking, "what would it take to get them to turn around, go back to France, and come back a few days later? That would give me another ten or twelve days of good eating."

Of course, New York harbor meant a lot more than that. Sure, there was the Statue of Liberty and all that it stood for. But it's funny how in a big new situation, some surprising things strike you. For example, the New York buildings. In Europe there were pictures of the skyline, and the pictures were black and white. And then you actually see the buildings and they're different *colors*. And you say to yourself, well, of course, they'd be different colors. But somehow, it's still a surprise.

Well, as an American citizen, I didn't have to go through that Ellis Island stuff. No sir. I walked ashore with all the other Americans. I wanted to think I looked like them. But even in my best Kolbuszowa suit, maybe I stood out a little. I know my suitcase stood out. Besides the few clothes I had brought, there was some cheese I thought might make a nice gift for a few relatives. Two weeks of travel from Kolbuszowa had added to its aging. I got some funny looks but I didn't really care. I was in America.

I lived with my uncle Martin's family on South Fifth Street in the Northside section of Williamsburg, Brooklyn. That whole section—Williamsburg and Greenpoint—was pretty well established as a place for Polish immigrants to get a start. That's where my father had gotten started.

Living with the family of my father's youngest brother was so typical of Polish immigrants. My father had brought Martin to America when he was a young man. Incidentally, a few years after he came to America, Martin—we always called him Stryj*—joined Pilsudski's Legions and fought the Russians. In fact, I remember that in 1919 while serving with the Legion, Stryj visited our farm in Kolbuszowa. He came back to settle in America, but like many Polish Americans, he

---

*In Polish, Stryj means uncle on your father's side. Wujek means uncle on your mother's side. A useful distinction.

cared passionately about Poland for the rest of his life. Stryj and his wife Stryjna were wonderful to me and to our family all the years we were struggling.

Anyway, when I got here the main thing was to learn English fast. So I signed up for night school and that was a big help. But you know what was even better? I had some young friends who had come from Poland a few years before and they were really into English. So to run with them, I had to pick it up as they talked. We were a bunch of guys about twenty years old, all in some kind of, what do you call it now, entry-level work, and having the best of both worlds—Polish cooking and American opportunity.

It may seem strange, but we brought no sports or games with us from Poland. I guess that's because we never really had much leisure time in Poland. So in America, when we did get a little leisure time, most us got interested in American sports, especially baseball and football. A few guys were also into boxing and running. It's funny, through the young people, some of the older folks became interested in American sports too. We were a kind of bridge for them.

We had other kinds of recreation too. We formed a Polish Falcons social club and had dances and picnics and nights where we played cards or just stood around the piano and sang old Polish and new American songs. We had sweaters and membership cards with the white birds on them, and we had officers and a headquarters on North Eighth Street—the whole thing. We had about fifty members. We even had a few members who were "straight" Americans, no Polish ancestry. They loved the sweaters, so we let them in as long as they lived up to the rules, which was easy.

There were a lot of other Polish American organizations that we tied into. The New National Hall in Greenpoint was a club where a lot of these groups had dances and other affairs. Any city where you find a lot of Polish Americans you'll find a New National Hall, or maybe several. These were the organizations that were established even before my father came here in 1903.

Then we had our "trips." We would travel all the way to Coney Island to go swimming, or to Maspeth for a picnic —usually an hour or so on the trolley car.

There were also a lot of young girls, factory workers, who had come from Poland and they were in these things too. One of the girls I went to school with in Poland, Mary Vargacki, was in this group and she met a good friend of mine from the club, Frank Tyburczy, the son of my godfather. They got married and I still hear from them once in awhile. It was all great fun and something I had never known in Poland.

I didn't run into much discrimination. I guess the earlier immigrants paid that price or maybe it was because in the first few years I was kind of sheltered, working and living among my own kind. Sure, once in awhile, when you'd mix with other kinds of people, you might hear "greenhorn" or something like that. But we didn't pay much attention and a lot of times it was said in fun.

MY FIRST JOB here, almost right off the boat, was as an electrician's helper. I didn't know much about electricity, but I had two things going for me. In 1927, there was a lot of work in New York converting the old gaslights to electricity so they needed able-bodied men with a little common sense who would work hard and learn fast. The other thing was that there was a pretty strong, what would you call it, "network," of Polish-Americans who looked out for each other. So a friend got me a job and I made $10 a week.

Pretty soon, some friends told me that I could get $16 a week where they worked, at the nearby Standard Manufacturing factory making clothes hampers and baskets. I jumped at it because I was already thinking about how to bring my brothers over from Poland. I worked eight-and-a-half hours a day, five-and-a-half days a week, as a sprayer's helper. Later, I became a sprayer for $24 a week. With overtime, I sometimes made $40; I was in, how do the kids say it, "fat city" money-wise, but the job was very tough, and not too healthy. That lasted until 1930 when the Depression really began to hit us all and a lot of us were thrown out of work.

Everybody knows that was a tough time. You had to get a break—and be willing to hustle and do manual work—to scratch out a living. One thing the Polish people had going for them is that they were savers, and not necessarily in banks. (I had saved a thousand dollars by 1930. Besides lending it to relatives, I paid for my brother Joe to come over from Poland in 1931.) So the people had a little to fall back on when the Depression hit. And they had a lot of pride. You didn't "go on relief" unless there was absolutely no other way. It was kind of a disgrace. So everybody was taking whatever jobs they could find, even temporary things. I worked for a little while helping to build the Holland Tunnel and I caddied out on Long Island. Then I got a break.

My mother's sister, Ciotka* Anna, a wonderful lady, was married to a hard-working man named Joe Straub who had built a small soda business in Brooklyn and "New York" (we always called Manhattan "New York" or "the city"). He asked me to join the business as a routeman—a deliverer and salesman on several routes. I'd have to learn how to drive a

*Ciotka is aunt on mother's side, Stryjna is aunt on father's side.

pretty good-sized truck and the work was tough—delivering a few hundred cases of soda every day and bringing back the empties—but it sounded like something secure. So I joined Straub Beverages in 1930.

Before long, I had a chance to buy and run my own Straub routes. I didn't hesitate. It was a chance to be my own boss, an independent businessman. I'd buy the soda from Straub and sell it to the customers that I built up. And a lot of that had to do with being Polish—there were a lot of Polish owners of groceries, "candy stores" and bars in various parts of Brooklyn and Queens. Of course, you had to give them good service. I would work from seven in the morning until I was finished, usually about six at night but later than that in the summer months, six days a week. And carrying boxes of twelve quarts of soda up, or down, a few flights of stairs was no picnic. But it was my business, so it was okay.

I met your mother at Straub's. Sophie was about eighteen, just a little out of high school and working as a $10-a-week bookkeeper there. Her mother used to give her a 25¢ a day allowance, 10¢ for carfare to and from South Brooklyn where they lived, and 15¢ for lunch. Our first "date" was when I took her out for lunch at the corner diner. She thought I was a big spender when I insisted that she take the "blue plate special"—pork chops, mashed potatoes, peas and carrots. It set me back 35¢, but it was an investment that has held up pretty well for 47 years of marriage.

WHEN WE GOT MARRIED in 1932, we had $200. We took a cold-water flat in Greenpoint, on Diamond Street, right down the block from Stryj and Stryjna's house, and a half block from St. Stanislaus Kostka church where my mother and father were married and I had been baptized.

Before we got married, though, there were some delicate "negotiations." You see, your mother was raised in the Polish *National* Church. A lot of people don't realize that within the Polish-American religious community there was a bit of competition. The Polish National Church had been formed here in America about the turn of the century. It was started by Polish Catholics who thought that "American" bishops weren't very sensitive to Polish parishes. So they set up their own bishop. We got married at Holy Cross Polish National Church in South Brooklyn and from then on practiced at Roman Catholic churches. Holy Cross was your mother's parish, in another of Brooklyn's Polish neighborhoods.

Her parents—the Machnichs—had come from Poland when they were young. He came from Przemysl in the east and she from Poznan in the west.

We were married on Saturday and on Monday I was back on the job at Straub's. We lived in that first flat a year and you were born there. The apartment was alright, but when Stryj and Stryjna told us that a flat was available in their house, we moved right in. Looking back now, neither place was all that fancy but at the time they were grand. And living in the same house with Stryj and Stryjna's family was great. You got "instant" brothers and sisters and plenty of loving care from Stryjna. You know, I've seen in newspapers that some experts now think it's good to have, how do they put it, an "extended family." Well a lot of Polish families, and I bet other immigrant families, had such strong ties that they were practicing that idea a long time before someone put a label on it.

We brought Tony over in late 1933 and, thanks again to

the Polish American "network" he got a job as a plumber pretty quickly. By then Joe had "paid his dues" by working in a button and novelty factory and was doing pretty well in a meat provisions plant. In 1935, we borrowed a little money to bring Ray from Poland. All my brothers, even Adam when he came over in 1939, lived with us until they got settled. Things were pretty tight, so your mother got a job at the Greenpoint jute mill. She probably wouldn't have gotten it, except there were still some people there who remembered my father as a manager. Later on, she worked at the Leviton electric switch plant in Greenpoint. And you spent more and more time with Stryjna and her family downstairs. You got so spoiled by her great cooking that it was hard to please you in our kitchen.

Just about then, something was beginning to happen with us and our friends. Looking at it now, it seems like it was more than just the usual thing of "wedding bells are breaking up that old gang of mine." Our friends were being spread out more than usual because in those days you went where the jobs were. So, soon after we were married and settled in Greenpoint, we saw friends moving to New Jersey, or Long Island or Connecticut—wherever there were jobs. That made it a little tougher to keep "our kind" together. Also, the new immigration laws, cutting down on people coming from places like Poland, were beginning to have an effect. There wasn't nearly as much "new stock" coming into the Polish American community.

Another thing: Some of us were getting a better look at the "outside." For me, the experience of running my own little business started me thinking about maybe a little bigger business. And I began to see a lot of homes with little pieces of ground around them. And I got to hear a lot of different points of view. I found that there were good and bad, smart and not-so-smart, in all groups. So why be afraid to mingle and play in a bigger ballpark?

Little by little some of us were getting "Americanized." And mainly that meant that we wanted what other Americans had, if not for ourselves then for our children. If it meant that eventually you might have to leave a Polish American community like Greenpoint to get it, well, that wouldn't be the end of the world.

Some people disagreed with that. They wanted to stay with their own. I can understand that. I can understand people wanting to belong to a church where they can worship in the only language they really know, or where the religious customs of the old country are preserved. In Brooklyn we had all kinds of ethnic churches. Remember, my parents travelled a couple of miles to Greenpoint to worship at St. Stanislaus even though there was "an Irish" church a few blocks away. And sometimes there were "Italian," Lithuanian," you name it, churches—all Catholic—a few blocks from each other. It wasn't very efficient, but that's what the people wanted. They wanted it so much that they would work very hard to build their church and sacrifice a lot to keep it going. Their heritage was that important to them.

Maybe these people were afraid they'd lose something precious. I still run into people who think they're living in "Poland in America." I try to tell them that if they would only let loose a little, become *Americans from Poland*, they could gain a lot. And of course, this applies to other ethnic groups too. I still have everything I brought from Poland—a sense of a tradition, a religion, values. But I've added a lot more in the years I've been here and all of it is what America gave me.

So back in the thirties, some people stayed "in the circle" while for some of us, there was something else opening up, and we took advantage of it.

COLORFUL CHARACTERS? Boy, Brooklyn had 'em in those days.

Did I ever tell you how I bought my 1927 bulletproof Marmon sedan?

One day a little after I joined Straub Beverages, a guy right out of an Edward G. Robinson movie comes in and says, "Anybody wanna buy a car?" Well, the other guys had cars and I had just learned to drive but hadn't gotten a car yet, so I said, "What have you got?"

He takes me outside and shows me something I couldn't believe. It was an aluminum-body Marmon, maybe twenty feet long. It must have weighed about the same as a pocket battleship. The guy says "I'll take $25 for it." So we drove it around the block and I bought it.

Later on I found out that the windows were bullet-proof and the engine had *sixteen* cylinders. "Yeah," a mechanic told me, "Eight work at one time while the other eight rest. They're sort of like spares." When I'd take it the twenty miles to Rockaway with a full tank of gas, I'd have to fill it up again to get home. The guy who sold it to me was a West Coast union rep for Harry Bridges' outfit. He was "on the lam."

Then there was Pete McGuinness. Pete was an oldtime politician who had dominated the 15th Assembly District in Brooklyn for years. He was the Democratic district leader and since there was no serious Republican Party there, Pete ran the whole political ballgame in and around Greenpoint. As leader and water commissioner, he controlled quite a few jobs at a time when people needed jobs desperately. He even has a street named for him in the heart of Greenpoint. Maybe because he called the place "The Gardenspot of the World."

Pete knew all the tricks. He could break your heart singing Irish tenor if you happened to be of that background. Or he could use straight political muscle if that was the best way to get what he wanted. He was heavy-set, with a big red face and blue eyes, and always smiling. He looked like one of the politicians in a movie I saw many years ago, "The Last Hurrah."

Well, the Polish people in Greenpoint felt for a long time that the Democratic Party was dominated by the Irish (who, after all, had worked hard for many years to get that control). There were two Polish Democratic Clubs in Greenpoint. Each club had about a hundred members. When I started to feel a little secure in business and the community, about 1935, I got active in the Polish Consolidated Democratic Club.

A couple years later, we actually defeated Pete's candidate for the Assembly with a Polish candidate.* But Pete moved quickly and kept a lot of control by sharing the patronage with us.

I've never regretted the time I spent at that club. I learned a lot about this political system, a good system. Eventually, I was president of the club. We put on voter registration drives, get-out-the-vote drives and all the other bread-and-butter political things that you have to do to win elections. And the

*Still later, our distant cousin, Chester Straub Jr., represented Greenpoint and neighboring sections of Brooklyn as Assemblyman. In recent years, a Greenpoint resident active in St. Stanislaus, Tom Bartosiewicz, has been serving as State Senator.

club helped people with a lot of day-to-day problems like citizenship papers, and taught people to read and write English.

It was a little bit like some of those scenes in "The Godfather." Poor immigrants who didn't understand the system and didn't know anyone in power. They needed a helping hand. The club tried to give it.

You know how powerful those ethnic political clubs were? We even had a *statewide* association of Polish Democratic clubs. We had state conventions at great places like Utica (I remember how proud I was the first time I went to one as the club's delegate). Democratic candidates for governor and senator used to come and address us.

All of that convinced me that if you want something in this country, you can organize and work for it and you have a good chance of getting it. So I can see why some newer immigrant groups are doing it now. And it's fine, as long as there's no violence or other off-base activity.

But by the 1940's, I was getting the itch to own my own home. In 1943, I had saved another $1,000 and we used it as a down payment for our first home, a $3,300 one-family house on a 60 x 100 foot plot in the suburbs at St. Albans, Queens. It was the end of my political "career," but the start of a lot of other things, including a "victory garden" of vegetables which reminded me a little of farming back in Poland.

America has been bountiful. "Other things" have included: two children who had access to a college education and the opportunities John never had, and twelve grandchildren who also have a social and economic base more secure than their grandfather's.

A "little bigger business" turned out to be a luncheonette in Flushing, Queens, run successfully with brother Joe for twenty years. The first house in Queens gave way to a succession of larger, more valuable properties until he and Sophie now enjoy—bask in— retirement in their St. Petersburg, Florida home and own another nearby.

And, finally, in the summer of 1979, it would mean a visit to Poland.

CHAPTER FOUR

John L. (1933–)

"KELLY, IN THIS SCHOOL WE SPEAK POLISH."
It's one of my earliest memories. It was one of many that
came flooding back to me when I visited the old
neighborhood, Greenpoint, Brooklyn, just before we
left for Poland. The half-hour drive from our Old West-
bury, Long Island, home ends with passage over the
Kosciuszko Bridge which for me links not only Brooklyn
and Queens but an old life and a new one.

The first memories were of the Diamond Street
coldwater flat above Stryj and Stryjna's. It was more
than alright to us then, but by our current standards it
was hardly plush.

For the younger folks who don't know what a
"coldwater flat" means, think of it literally. The house
had no central heating system. No warm air. No hot
water. I remember that as a pre-schooler on wintry days
I'd stay huddled under our thick Polish comforter (a
pierzyna) in an unheated bedroom until my mother
wrapped me in a blanket and carried me into the kitchen.
There, a gas burner would be heating the water and

50

throwing off just enough warmth to take the chatter off my teeth.

The 15-foot square kitchen was an all-purpose room. It was the social center for the family and visitors (only on special occasions did we invite guests into the "frontroom," a living room so named because it was at the head of the railroad-room layout of the flat and faced the *front* of the house and the street below). Of course, we ate our meals in the kitchen too. And on the many evenings when there weren't any guests, it was where we did our homework, listened to the radio or just sat and talked.

Our kitchen in the Diamond Street flat had something else that may seem a bit peculiar to the more affluent younger generation. It was the site of our bathtub in which we washed clothes, linens and bodies. Since the entrance to the flat was through the kitchen, this occasionally presented a ticklish social situation.

Summers in the flat were not pleasant. Attached to other tenements on both sides, there was no cross ventilation. And the pavement in the street below seemed to absorb heat in the day and release it at night. There wasn't a tree on the entire block. "Air conditioning" meant a fan—not an electric fan, the kind you hold and wave. But we made do.

One thing that made life in Greenpoint fun for young boys was the street sports. I played "ball" as early as I can remember. But it wasn't baseball. The nearest honest-to-goodness baseball field—with real dirt and grass—was in McCarran Park, about a half a mile away, and I couldn't even cross the street without permission.

So we played stoopball. You'd throw a pink "spaldeen" rubber ball off the steps of the stoop,* and depending on where it landed and if it was fielded cleanly by your opponent, you got a man on base or an "out." The trick was to hit the point of a step so the ball would carom out of reach of the fielder, perhaps into home run territory.

More ingeniously, you could use the cracks in the sidewalk to play "boxball." In this micro-stadium, you simply tapped the ball with an open hand into your opponent's box and waited for him to do likewise. Interminable boredom, but it often kept us from asking "Ma, what is there to do?"

When you were old enough to use the street itself for sports, you graduated to punchball and stickball. Punchball was a variation of baseball, wherein, fittingly enough, you punched a rubber ball instead of hitting it with a bat. (And slapball was a variant of punchball, where the hand had to be held open when meeting the ball; you could put all kinds of "flukes" on the ball if you "sliced" it just right.) Stickball was baseball with a broomstick. You could play it with five or six on a side, over the length of the street, or, with two players using a "strike zone" painted on the side of an empty building (after agreeing to how far the ball had to be hit to earn a single, double, triple or homer). A lot of garage owners

*When I first mentioned stoopball to my children, they didn't know what a "stoop" was. A stoop is a set of four or five stairs, usually brick or concrete, leading to the entrance of the house.

on Diamond Street were involuntary hosts for stickball "strike zones."

Finally, there was Chinese handball, again played against a garage wall or other flat surface. It was one of the more common causes of being chased by grown-ups unsympathetic to our needs for energy outlets.

When I visited Diamond Street in 1979, "no ball playing" signs still seemed to be on many of the best stickball walls, and the kids seemed to pay as much attention to them as we did. Another thing struck me about Diamond Street in 1979. Cars lined both sides of the street. When we lived there in the late 'thirties and early 'forties, there were only three or four cars parked randomly on the entire block.

And incredibly, the sidewalk and front of the house across the street where we were always chased from playing still looked immaculate thirty-seven years after the fact. Many of my pals had "died" with me on that sidewalk, "electrocuted" by the evil "witch" who owned that immaculate property.

And in 1979 I walked the length of Diamond Street, marvelling at the fact that the houses were not nearly as tall or as wide as I had remembered them. The empty store on the corner of Norman Avenue returned in my mind's eye as the old "beer garden" with its occasional customer striding home with that era's version of the six-pack, a quart bucket of draft beer. And the kids who lived or played on the block came back too—many of them "Polish," but others like Freddy Schwartz and Willy Shaplin and Petey Rago. Passing the house where

I was born and the house where I spent my early childhood, I wondered who inhabited them. Would they be as lucky as I and my family have been?

Another thing: It was difficult to find a home that hadn't been remodeled recently. These buildings, many of them a hundred years old, were almost all spic and span. I was told that it's the result of a continual influx of immigrants, from Poland and other parts of the world, who have worked hard, saved their money and purchased the homes. Proud of these homes, the relatively new residents, along with the children and grandchildren of earlier residents have kept this section of Greenpoint from the kind of absentee ownership that seems to have blighted many other parts of New York and other older American cities.

I passed some stores whose owners were anxious to serve recent immigrants. They displayed signs that speak volumes: Right next to "Mówimy po Polsku" was "Hablamos Espanol."

SZKOŁA SWIĘTEGO STANISLAWA, to give St. Stanislaus School its proper Polish name, was a special place. For me, it was the central fact of "growing up ethnic." The parish was established in 1896 by Polish immigrants. By 1904, the cornerstone of an imposing twinspired church was laid and the Polish American community in the northern part of Brooklyn had a place to worship the way they had in the old country. Since the founding of St. Stanislaus, a Polish pastor had been in charge and curates who spoke Polish were always available to hear confessions or simply offer consolation in the old tongue.

St. Stanislaus' "old school" was a four-story concrete-faced structure with ten classrooms and a few administrative offices. It was staffed by the Sisters of the Holy Family of Nazareth. The Order attracted young Polish American women with a vocation to teach the Catholic religion, the Polish language and the basics of education to Polish American youth and anyone else who would accept this hierarchy of subject matter.

Almost all of the children who attended St. Stanislaus were quite prepared to accept it because they came from Polish American families. I've recovered a list of my first grade companions at St. Stanislaus, Sister Gonzelva's class of 1939–40. It goes like this:

Bode, Brzozowska, Czartoryski, Danielewski, Fromalc, Ghez, Gregorek, Gregorek, Grzymko, Gunstone, Hoffman, Jablonski, Jones (Stanislas), Kowalska, Kozakiewicz, Leistschitzky, Malek, Nowak, Nurkiewicz, Paluszek, Portor, Potrzeba, Sendrowski, Staskowski, Solas, Trzcinski, Urbanski, Wezkiewicz, Wilantewicz, Zubrzycki.

We spoke English at home. But I had been exposed to Polish in Stryj and Stryjna's house, during visits to my mother's parents and whenever we'd have visitors. So the formal introduction to the language at St. Stanislaus was more of a strengthening of what my young absorbent mind had already picked up. Still, basic understanding was one thing and speaking the language something else again. There must be something genetic in being able to pronounce sounds like "sz," "cz," and even "szcz" properly. The necessary arrangement of tongue, teeth and roof of mouth are something that has taken nature at least a thousand years to make possible. Poles in Poland, of course, can do it with ease. Some Polish Americans can and some can't. But try to teach a young Irish American or Italian American how to do it and, no matter how smart the child is, you're fighting genetics.

So, hardly a day would go by when, after sing-songing the Polish alphabet for a half-hour (ah, beh, ceh, deh, eh, efff, ge, ha . . .) we'd go into pronounciation drills and one of the "gentically deprived" would run into trouble.

"Kelly,* in this school we speak Polish. And if you don't care to learn it, you can go to the *public* school," Sister would say. The word "public" was usually delivered with a condemnatory sneer. In those days, our parents were supposed to send us to Catholic school if at all possible under the penalty of damnation. We all knew that some of the kids in the public school might be saved but after listening to the Sisters' descriptions of Hell, very few of us wanted to take any chances. In training for First Communion (which, incidentally came rather late at St. Stanislaus—in the fourth grade) the "publics"

*Name changed to protect the innocent.

and the "Catholics" had different schedules and separate seating assignments.

WHEN GERMANY INVADED POLAND in September, 1939, to us it was as if a part of America had been violated.

In those days, every week St. Stanislaus published *The Patron*, a 16-page magazine (24 or 30 pages at Christmas and Easter). Soon *The Patron* was carrying stories headlined, "German Treatment of Women in Poland," "German Morale is Breaking in Poland" and "Poland Seen Key to Lasting Peace." About half the articles were in Polish and half in English.

After America entered the war, there were all kinds of patriotic features along with news of the boys overseas and, inevitably, the tragic notice of a son lost in battle.

But culture persisted even during the war. *The Patron* sponsored a series of "musicales" including Pagliacci, Aida and Carmen. And there were articles on Joseph (Conrad) Korzeniowski and "My Mother Was Polish" by Ewa Curie. Plus some good advice: "Go See 'Madame Curie' at the Radio City Music Hall."

What I liked best was the way the old Polish customs were described. At the time of the Wielkanoc (Easter) celebration, I learned how "Dyngus" Monday, the day after Easter, was celebrated in Poland. On that day every year, the boys in the villages were permitted to duck the girls in the water of the nearest brook. I knew a few I would have liked to practice on.

THEN THERE WERE THE DODGERS. In 1941, Brooklyn was consumed by their transformation from clowns to champs (they would be re-incarnated in 1969 in the New York Mets and my children could partake in what I had experienced as an eight-year-old.)

Those were the days when baseball players were giants. Even their names were thrilling. Has there ever been an array of ballplayers like those on the 1941–42 Dodgers? Can any team match Dixie (Walker), Ducky (Medwick), Arky (Vaughn), Cookie (Lavagetto), Frenchy (Bordagaray) and Pee Wee (Reese)—all of them conducted through unspeakable dangers by Leo the Lip (Durocher). Today, many of the stars have names like Robin, Lance and Darrell.

For me, the Catholic education at St. Stanislaus and the community worship of the Dodgers came together at a particularly impressionable age. Shortly after the good sisters impressed upon me the need to remain in the state of grace ("you could die in your sleep, you know") I was promised a seat at a Dodger-Braves doubleheader at Ebbets Field. I remember my prayer at bedtime the night before this historic event: "Lord, don't let me die in my sleep tonight. Let me see Whitlow Wyatt and Curt Davis pitch tomorrow and if You want, I'll go peacefully tomorrow night."

Of course, we didn't spend *all* of our time in Brooklyn. Dad saw to it that my mother and I spent some time during the summer "out of the hot city." So we spent two summers on the farm of a wonderful family, Ted and Betty Brelsford at Ringoes, New Jersey,

58

about sixty miles away. That was always fun, but what was even more interesting was our exchange of Christmas gifts with the Brelsfords. Mom would send some clothes for the kids. They would send us freshly-slaughtered chickens. Whenever the bloodied packages arrived, the mailman and neighbors wondered whether we were members of some obscure religious cult.

Sometimes I would "go out on the route" with my father. First the truck had to be loaded at the soda bottling plant. Impressions of an eight year old remain: The smell of the plant—a mixture of cork from the bottle caps, the wood of the cases, the oil lubricating the bottling machinery, sugar and other soda ingredients. And the rhythmic noise as the endless line of bottles took their fill of wildly colored fluids, hesitated momentarily before being capped, and surrendered to the twelve-bottle cases.

Watching Dad carry a few hundred cases of soda into cellars or to the upper floors of Polish National Halls was probably the seed for my interest in a college education. When he began to suggest that I go to college so I could "work with my head," any inclination to resist was long gone.

GRAMPA MACHNIC was a forbidding presence. He was not the kind to hoist you on his knee. He was tall and heavy and spoke gruffly. I was afraid of him. I think everyone was afraid of him. But ever since I could remember, on Sundays we would visit him and Granma in their Bay Ridge home. Bay Ridge was another

59

Polish American neighborhood, down in south-central Brooklyn, about a half-hour's drive.

The Sunday visits would usually begin in early afternoon and last until late at night. Grampa and Dad would share a bottle of Four Feathers or Old Overholt for an hour or two while my mother and grandmother finished preparing the multi-course dinner. After dinner, in the overheated living room, Grampa and Dad would doze for an hour or two while the women took care of the clean up. This was the time for my forbidden pleasure—a few taps on Aunt Frances' typewriter, off-limits to me, and all the more tempting because of it.

Most of those Sunday nights, the second phase began at 9 P.M. with Gabriel Heater, the radio commentator who sounded like the voice of the apocalypse. I didn't follow much of what he had to say to Grampa and Dad and other listeners, but I was always impressed with his opening: "Ah, there's good news (or bad news) tonight!" The bad-news nights seemed to outnumber the good-news nights by about three to one.

Sometimes, phase-two of the Sunday visit was quite different. We'd all get into Dad's 1936 Olds—its gently rounded front fenders and heavy-lidded headlights combining to resemble the face of a highborn beauty—and we'd drive down to Holy Cross Church on Fifteenth Street. There, some Sundays, you could see an amateur drama group do an all-Polish play on how well or how poorly immigrants and their families were doing in their adopted land. Much more fun, though, were the Sunday night dances at the hall—a Polish band playing a seemingly endless stream of polkas, obereks and other old-country favorites, with young and old alike dancing with reckless abandon late into the night. (At a Polish American festival in 1979, I heard a middle-aged man wonder aloud, "My grandmother could do those polkas all night long without losing her breath, so how come I'm exhausted after just one dance?")

Grampa Machnic was always pretty clear on what he wanted and what he didn't want. For one thing, he wanted all of his children to marry Polish Americans. That's the way it worked out with the two older children, my mother and my uncle John. But the younger daughter, Frances, had other ideas. She met and grew fond of a fine young Jewish lad. Grampa would have none of it, not even allowing Frances' beau to pick her up at the house, so my uncle Tony occasionally functioned as a decoy escort. It was all very uncomfortable, and Frances eventually married Sam despite Grampa's unbending condemnation. I sometimes wonder how he would have felt about his grandchildren's marriages. I have a feeling that if he lived, he would have boycotted this grandson's wedding in 1955 to Jean Murphy. It would have hurt a bit, but certainly once again it would have been in vain.

WE LEFT GREENPOINT AND OUR POLISH ROOTS when I was almost ten. By then, Dad was moving us more fully into the absorption process and at the same time improving our standard of living. Instead of the cold-water flat, we had a two-story house in suburban St. Albans, Queens, all to ourselves. Three bedrooms meant I had one for myself. A living room, dining room and kitchen on the main floor meant plenty of room to entertain with no bathtub in the kitchen to delay visitors. Central heating. And we had *land*! The house stood on a 60 x 100-foot plot, which left room for a small garage, a modest Victory Garden of vegetables and a compact front lawn.

The move from Greenpoint was no great joy for me. Leaving all the good friends was bad enough. But adjusting to a new school presented some special problems. First, it was about twelve blocks away, a distance we walked in all kinds of weather.

But my big problem with this school and the parish that ran it, St. Pascal Baylon, was that it was "Irish." That meant mainly that the priests and sisters were of Irish descent, as were a majority of the parishioners. Well, in this school they did some peculiar things, like saying their prayers in English. Here I was, ten years old and in the fifth grade, and it became obvious to my classmates that I couldn't say my prayers. I didn't try to explain. I just learned fast.

Of course some of the problems I had at St. Pascal's had more to do with dawning adolescence than absorption into the American mainstream. I can remember a time in the seventh grade when, having noticed girls for the first time, I decided to start neatening up. One morning in the bathroom, I was desperate for something to use as hair tonic. I grabbed a likely-looking bottle, applied the contents, and left for school. It was bad luck that just as I got to the schoolyard and met the gang, it started to rain. Before I could get to shelter my head was a mass of frothy bubbles, my "hair tonic"—shampoo—having proved very effective. The girls loved it.

By contrast with my first class at St. Stanislaus, my classmates at St. Pascal's presented a little more of an ethnic mosaic. There were about ninety students in that class, not uncommon in the Catholic elementary schools of that day. The good sisters were somehow—miraculously?—able to keep that kind of herd in order, teach them the essentials and inspire them to persevere in the Catholic faith. Of course some of the good sisters were just a bit eccentric. I remember one who expected her eighty students to mount three flights of stairs without a single sound, like spies stealthily scaling an enemy wall. One sound and there was a cuff to the head. But she was a hell of a math teacher.

High school was relatively uneventful. I attended the local public school, Andrew Jackson, and got my first social exposure to blacks and Jews. It was all rather smooth.

In that period, two events made a lasting impression —I read a book and got a job.

The book was "You Can Change the World" by Father Keller, the founder of the Christophers movement. I was about seventeen and Father Keller was telling me that depending on my outlook, career choice, energy and luck, I could make a difference. He wrote that in careers like communications and personnel relations, a well-motivated, hard working man or woman could change things, make the world a better place. For this impressionable adolescent about to start college, the book came at just the right time.

Just about then, I got a summer job in the shipping department of McGraw-Hill Book Company "in the city." It was eight hours of drudgery, filling mail pouches with packages of one or several books. A big clock right over our packing station was obstinate; it's hands rarely moved. But the worst time of the day was at mid-morning when I became the shipping department's "gofer" to the company coffee shop. Wearing soiled working clothes, standing dirty and sweaty, I would take my place in line with all the "gofers" from the company's white-collar departments, most of them young women about my age, dressed and groomed meticulously. Total mortification. And confirmation in the resolution to "work with my head" in the years to come, just like Dad suggested.

COLLEGE WAS SOMETHING ELSE. I was the first in my family to go to college. I was the first to get the chance to "work with my head" rather than with my hands. Of course, what we've come to call blue-collar work is no less noble, no less necessary than what I do. But it *is* different. And in most cases, blue-collar workers do not get a chance for as much economic reward or social mobility as do those of us who work in managerial, academic or professional positions.

But if I've achieved anything, it's due first to the

platform my parents built for me; then to the totally supportive role of my wife in raising our family and running the household (husband-wife roles were a lot clearer when we married); and, finally, the motivation and knowledge added by the college I attended.

There are several dozen colleges, mainly in our large cities, that have played an especially important role in helping generations of low-income and middle-income, ethnically-oriented students to move substantially upward in American social structure. I know one such school intimately, Manhattan College in New York City, but I suspect that a number of colleges in New York and other cities like Boston, Philadelphia, Chicago, St. Louis, Houston, Phoenix, Los Angeles and San Francisco have similar track records.*

Many of these schools have been run by religious orders, people who have dedicated their lives to helping students. These educators have encouraged the fullest development of abilities and have suggested a point of view concerning this society. They have helped their students think, "Hey, I can run with these guys,"—meaning the "establishment"—and yet have compassion for the less fortunate. They have taught us how to think and how to feel.

And that, essentially, is *my* story.

*This is not to disparage other colleges and universities that have contributed to Americans' upward mobility—for example, the great land-grant universities. However, the students I'm writing about have been centered mainly in the larger cities and, until relatively recently, could not afford to "go away to college."

END OF REVERIE.

It was summer, 1979.

After many years of wondering what Poland is like, what our family farm and village are like, how the people there think and how they live—it was almost time to go. The airline tickets and hotel reservations were in hand.

As a "warm-up" we went to the Polish American museum in nearby Port Washington and to the annual Polish Festival at "Polish Town" in Riverhead, Long Island. At Riverhead, there was: Polka music and dancing all day long with bands like "Stanky and the Coal Miners" and "The New Sound;" Polish food at booths all up and down Riverhead's Pulaski Street and adjoining streets; Polish arts and crafts and souvenirs ("Take something home for Stasiu, Jasiu and Uncle Ziggy!"); "Miss Polish Town;" and thousands of happy people.

The banners proclaimed, "Witamy" (Welcome).

We'd soon see the same banners in Poland, the root of all this tradition and merriment.

AN AMERICAN
JOURNEY

"Hold on to your culture. Keep it alive. Let it be your gift to the world."

Pope John Paul II, speaking to a vast throng of Ghanians during his May, 1980, trip to Africa.

CHAPTER ONE

WE WENT TO POLAND, my father and I.

Exactly one year before Solidarity, one year before the beginning of a critical new period in Polish history —perhaps in world history as well—we got a glimpse of the forces at work in that courageous, oppressed country.

What began as a return to personal roots soon took on additional significance, a significance we couldn't fully appreciate until the events of 1980 and 1981 began to unfold.

Yes, we went to Poland, my father and I, and saw much more than we had anticipated. Dad was returning after fifty-two years. And I was about to get my first look at a land and a people both foreign and familiar, never seen but often imagined. He was curious to see how much the country had changed. I was curious to see whence we had come.

On the eve of our departure, four of my father's brothers came to our Long Island home. Joe had come from Florida with Dad, Tony from a short stay in

Holland, Adam from Detroit and Jacob had just arrived on a visit from Poland. It was the first time the five brothers had been together, Jacob having been born after Dad left for America. They talked of old days on the farm and new days in America, of families grown and dispersed, and of what was yet to be. There were toasts and farewells.

It would take Dad and I 13 hours to travel from Long Island to Warsaw. When he left Poland in 1927, it had taken him 13 *days* to travel the same distance.

POLAND IS A NATION OF 35 MILLION people who live in an area about the size of Ohio, Indiana and Kentucky. It borders the Baltic Sea, the Soviet Union, Czechoslovakia and East Germany. Except for the Carpathian Mountains along the Czech border, the land is mainly flat. The climate is not unlike northeastern United States. The Polish economy is still agriculturally-based (wheat, rye, oats, potatoes, sugar beets and livestock), but urbanization and pocket industrialization is increasing rapidly; mining, iron and steel production, chemical processing, textile manufacturing, and food processing are all growth industries.

Warsaw, Poland's capital and largest city, has about 1½ million inhabitants. Cracow, the ancient capital, in the south central part of the country, is the cultural and historical soul of the nation. The mighty Vistula River, the nation's chief waterway, links the two cities.

We spent two weeks touring Warsaw, Cracow and the southern third of the country. We travelled by air and rail but mostly by car. Arrangements were handled by Aunt Sophie, Dad's sister, and her husband Jerzyk, both of whom accompanied us throughout our stay.

AS INTERNATIONAL TRAVELLERS, WE WERE "RUBES." Dad had been too busy earning a living all those years to travel abroad. And although I was a 45-year-old "sophisticated American businessman," I had never been to Europe.

We landed at "Warszawa" about mid-day. Careful security checks and lengthy currency exchange couldn't dampen the spirit. After all these years I was finally in this country I had heard so much about. I had a silly thought. "My God, I'm in Poland, surrounded by Poles!" Somehow hearing everyone talking in another language, even one I was somewhat familiar with, hit home. The feeling was even stronger when three little children, about four or five years old, walked by chattering in Polish. Their singsong voices made it all very real. *Children* talking Polish! (What did you expect, dummy? Would Polish kids talk English?)

WARSAW IS THREE CITIES. All relate to World War II. One part of the city, demolished during the war, has been painstakingly rebuilt. This is Stare Miasto (Old Town) and its environs.

Stare Miasto gave me my first feelings of the depth of the Polish heritage, feelings that would surface throughout the visit and beyond, perhaps forever.

Consider: On January 17, 1945, when Warsaw was

"liberated," the city was largely rubble. Of about 25,000 pre-war structures, only a few more than 4,000 survived. Stare Miasto, once the site of rows of handsome homes of burghers and adjoining historic castles and palaces, had been razed. But Varsavians pledged to rebuild the structures. And rebuild them they have with dedication to meticulous reproduction. The Rynek, or Square, was re-opened in 1953 and many other structures have been restored since then.

Warsaw's "crown jewel," literally and figuratively, is the Royal Castle—the beloved Zamek. The home of Polish kings, the seat of the 16th century parliament and the residence of presidents, Zamek is part of the Polish soul. Its restoration is now complete. Something in the Polish psyche can now rest. As the director of the restoration project has put it, "The castle is the symbol of our country, our nation, our whole history. It means that Poland is still alive."

The "second Warsaw" is the central business district. It too was rebuilt after the war. It is dull, drab, grey and chipping at the edges. Dozens of cement-faced buildings, eight or ten stories high, line streets broad and narrow. The buildings house the endless "bureaus"— government ministries—as well as commercial operations. It's understandable that the city had to be rebuilt quickly and economically after the war. But unfortunately, the buildings' design and materials produce a feeling of suppression. Precious few structures use color, glass or light. It is heavy in spirit.

The "third Warsaw" is that which remains from

72

before the war—quaint old buildings, many with impressive baroque architectural flourishes, some with bulletholes that remind you of what happened here.

The streets of Warsaw present other chilling reminders of the 1940s. On bustling Aleje Jerozolimskie in the heart of the city, a small memorial plaza stands at the front of the Hotel Forum. In the center of the plaza, there is red and white Polish bunting, a bouquet of flowers and a plaque that reads, "On this site on January 28, 1944, the Germans executed 102 Polish citizens."

There are *361* such memorial sites on Warsaw streets. On September 1st, the fortieth anniversary of the Nazi invasion of Poland, many of the plaques had lighted candles clustered about them. In other places around the city, such candles appeared mysteriously on sidewalks and in alleys. Varsavians remember the exact spot on which a relative or friend was shot.

Two blocks further east on Aleje Jerozolimskie, an unobtrusive wall plaque commemorates the site of the main barricade of the Warsaw Uprising of 1944. In the spring of that year, Polish partisans held off the German Army for 63 days. Inevitably, the Poles were wiped out.

SUNDAY MASS IN WARSAW made me think of St. Stanislaus in Greenpoint. We were at St. Ann's at the Square of the Three Crosses. The service was almost completely in Latin with some Polish hymns that I had long forgotten. Everyone sang with high spirit. The church was packed. There was a fair proportion of people of all ages. The mass we attended was one of six at the church that day. And St. Ann's is one of many churches in Warsaw.

In the churches we visited, the priests took up the collection. When a priest-collector looked me in the eye and said "God's blessings" I let go of some extra zloty. I hope this idea doesn't catch on in America.

For a few days we did the tourist bit: There was the quick drive to Warsaw's southern outskirts to King Jan Sobieski's Wilanow palace, an impressive structure for the impressive leader who defeated the Turks at Vienna. And in Warsaw itself, we visited Lazienki Park and within it the 17th century palace of Poland's last king, Stanislaus Augustus Poniatowski. The "island palace" stands astride a lake in the park and contains a dazzling array of medieval tapestries, antiques and artwork. We ignored the Soviet-built Palace of Culture, a brooding presence in the center of the city, but spent some time at the Tomb of the Unknown Soldier in Victory Square.

Fascinating as Warsaw was to two American visitors, it was time to leave for our village of Kolbuszowa and an even closer look at our Polish roots.

WE LANDED IN A CORNFIELD—by design. The airport at Rzeszow is about ten miles outside of this city of about 110,000 and right in the middle of a cornfield that would make an Iowan proud. We had flown about an hour in a Polish twin-engine prop-jet. No problem, it got us there.

The ride into town, on one of the ubiquitous, be-curtained Polish autobuses, was punctuated by religious mini-shrines along the roadsides and an occasional cow being "walked," very much the way American dogs are walked in the early evening.

Rzeszow was the intermediate point on our way to Kolbuszowa. As we walked a few blocks to the bus terminal, I had the uneasy feeling that we were being watched. Some Iron-Curtain-Country stories of the 'fifties flashed through my mind. Spies, being "tailed," the whole bit.

The juices were really flowing when I realized that we were being watched by just about *everybody*. Because Dad and I were obviously Americans. For the first time in my life, I found that my clothing had made me a celebrity.

Now, I am not known as a flashy dresser. My friends call me three-button-John and Mr. Conservative. But on the streets of Rzeszow, heads turned and remarks were stage-whispered (the one I liked best was "bogaty," meaning "rich man"). I tried to look casual in my three-button denim sports jacket, blue button-down shirt, paisley tie and tan levis. It was no use. I stood out like a rock star in Des Moines. (I had had a foretaste of this a few days before in Warsaw where my yellow Jack Nicklaus golf jacket apparently stamped me as a man to be watched by the thousands of people in many shades of gray.)

It was almost dusk, Sunday, August 26th, when we approached Kolbuszowa in the autobus. He hadn't been there for fifty-two years, but Dad knew every twist in the road. As we approached the town on Ulica Olszowe-

75

ga, he looked in vain for the old farmhouse. "It should be right about there . . ." he started to say, and then realized that three "new" homes and the growth of foliage now screened the old family farmhouse from view.

We debarked at the Kolbuszowa bus "terminal" a seedy compressed grouping of five small concrete buildings which, of course, hadn't been there when Dad left. The few dozen people milling around the terminal looked at us as if we were from another planet. I confess that I was beginning to think the same, but the glow of being where Dad had grown up, and where so many earlier generations of our family had lived and died, washed away everything else.

For the next few days, we explored Kolbuszowa and the neighboring village of Lipnica where he had spent much of his childhood.

"That furniture factory wasn't there and none of those houses. We used to be able to see from our house to the church in the village. That's about a mile away." He was taking a quick inventory before we went to pay our respects to friends and relatives.

"And now they've got a few building-supply factories and a shoe plant here. Looks like they're really trying to change the place.

"The square is different. (It had been demolished on September 9, 1939, as the German wave rolled through southeastern Poland. German artillery and Stuka dive bombers had softened it up; then mechanized units made it all too plain that the Polish cavalry was obsolete.)

76

"It used to be an open market for all kinds of vegetables and fruits and animals." The square, or "rynek," was rebuilt after the war with stores on the perimeter and a small park in the center. A monument erected by the Russians commemorating their dead in the 1944 campaign against the Germans stands virtually ignored in the center of the park.

ST. MARY'S CHURCH IN KOLBUSZOWA sits atop a small hill just off the rynek. It dominates the town. The first church was built in this town in 1523. Successor structures had come and gone until the "new" church was finished in 1933. The interior is impressive. Its liturgical art is well preserved. Large paintings of the Stations of the Cross and a recently added full-length portrait of Pope John Paul II dominate the inside. I was surprised at how wide the center aisle was.

The outside of the church was a disappointment. The cement facing had long ago turned into a shabby dark gray. The grounds were unkept (grass in Poland's public places seems to be cut even less frequently than in my backyard).

We were told that eight priests and six nuns ministered to the town's 5,000 parishioners. There are six masses on Sunday but none on Saturday, as in America.

All that didn't matter much when Dad and I stepped into the two-hundred-year-old cemetery behind the church. On this cool gray morning in late August, a son finally returned to his parents, and he brought *his* son.

The gravesite was raised slightly above those nearest

it. Mary Paluszek, (1889–1968), and Jozef Paluszek (1885–1969), rest there with their daughter Mary and her infant child.

For a few moments there was peace and continuity and fulfillment. If we did nothing else in Poland it would have been enough.

Later, he told me, "You know, I had so little time with my mother. And she was so young as a mother. She was only nineteen when I was born.

"They tell me that when I was about three, during the winter after she had just returned from America, we were at a wedding reception on a neighboring farm. It was one of those rare times when hard-working people could really enjoy themselves. She was dancing all through the evening and I had found a cozy spot to watch all the partying. I was sitting on the top of the big wall oven in the open kitchen. But it was getting too warm.

"Just after the music stopped, I yelled, 'Hey, Mary, get me off this stove before I bake!' "

"THE SCHOOHOUSE HASN'T CHANGED! How can that be? It's more than 65 years since I went to school here."

We were in Lipnica, the neighboring village, where Dad had grown up. He led the tour through what must have been a hundred-year-old structure. We entered one of the five classrooms.

"I can still see Mr. Piecara standing right here at the

head of the class. How old was I? Eight? Ten? My God, these could be the same desks." He took us through the hall and out onto the front steps. "Once, I tripped right here and bumped my head on this concrete railing. Look, I still have the scar."

Too soon, it was time to go. A class was leaving school. About a dozen girls, maybe in the fifth grade, lingered near the strangers. As Dad posed on the steps for a photo, an idea: "Young ladies, how would you like to go to America, in a picture?" Giggles and squeals. Then the grouping. In that frame, a span of three generations and two worlds.

WE FOUND THE OLD FARM HOUSE, but it wasn't easy.

Once again, it was the foliage and the "new" houses that screened the house, which was about 500 feet in from the roadside. Actually, we might not have found it at all if it wasn't for Mrs. Wiézek. The taxi had slowed down as directed and Dad had taken a stab at about where the house should be. His guess turned out to be Mrs. Wiézek's house, a thatched cottage surrounded by a picket fence that kept most of the livestock close to home.*

*A confirmed city boy, I had run into a mystery. As we walked among the small farms, it seemed to me that hundreds of chickens seemed to be wandering the land in small and large groups—mingling, breaking up and regrouping. "All the chickens look alike Dad. How do the people know which chickens they own?"

"It's not the people you know," he smiled, "it's the chickens. They know who feeds them."

I think I understand.

Mrs. Wiézek is a kindly old peasant lady with a sense of humor. As we introduced ourselves, she spotted a neighboring farmer strolling by. "Hey, Staś, come here," she called, "these people are visitors from America and they brought you a hundred dollars from your brother in Buffalo."

The craggy old man never broke stride. "You are pulling my leg, old woman. My brother, the cheapskate, hasn't sent me a dime in years. Those nice people are surely from America [the yellow golf jacket again], but they have nothing for me."

She remembered the Paluszeks "although it was many years ago that you left here." She directed us to the old family home about a quarter mile to the west.

It was dilapidated, unoccupied for maybe twenty years. But I could see how at one time it was an attractive, if compact, shelter for a small family. As the family increased, it obviously outgrew this place.

It was all wood. Some heavy timbers, about ten inches square, had been piled about ten feet high as the front wall. A mortar-like substance had been used to fill the spaces between the timbers. It looked not very different from the pictures of log cabins and other homes built on the American frontier in the 1800s. But the sharply pitched roof made of thick-hewn woodshakes made it indisputably an old Polish farm house.

"Come here, let me show you something," Dad said as he took a few steps toward the field. "Our crop land is right in front of you." What he was referring to was a narrow strip of land, which stretched, he said, about two miles westward. *But it was only about eighty feet wide.* I couldn't believe it.

"It's true. The whole system of land inheritance here over the centuries has cut these farms up into little strips.* When I left, all the farms were like this except those of the wealthy landowners, the hrabia and dziedzic. And there was no way they were going to part with their land."

This semi-feudal kind of land ownership made for inefficiencies that persist even today. "Look, you see the horse pulling the plow," Dad noted. "It's the same here now as it was when I left."

We were about to leave the old farm when he tugged at my arm. "Hey, I planted that apple tree. Look at all those apples!"

"THIS IS THE SPOT." Now we were in the church-yard of St. Mary's in Dziekowiec, a hamlet about half way between Lipnica and Kolbuszowa.

"We didn't have a church in Lipnica, so we had to walk about four miles every Sunday and holy day to this church. The people from about three or four neighboring villages all did that.

"This is the spot where I received confirmation. I'll never forget it. It was right under these big old trees. It was 1922 and I was about fourteen. My godfather was

---

*Later, when I reflected on the aerial views of Polish farmland, I realized how true this was. When you fly over American farmland, it looks like large rectangles of various shades and colors. But Polish farmland, from the air, looks like a parquet floor.

standing behind me—I can almost feel his hand on my shoulder—and the bishop came down the line and gave each of us a little slap and some kind of oil on the forehead."

It was the church where grandfather Jozef had been baptized almost 95 years earlier.

As the taxi took us back to Kolbuszowa, Dad's memory was stirred further.

"Look at those fields. Corn. We didn't grow corn when I was here. Now we're passing what used to be a big estate. The hrabia (a baron) here owned thousands of acres. I think the Russians sent him packing after the war and broke it up into small farms."

(I couldn't help thinking how differently we approached a somewhat similar objective in America. Long Island's north shore, where we live, had been called the "Gold Coast" for fifty or sixty years because of several hundred magnificent estates built there in the early 1900s. For the past twenty years or so, most of those estates have been broken up by developers; thousands of families now live in comfort where only a few hundred had lived in opulence.)

"This is the road I walked to get to church. About half way home, a little before the small pasture we owned, I used to stop at my aunt Eva's house and she'd fill me with some great pastry. Eva was married to a retired German Army man. They lived in a little German section of the village, maybe fifty families. I've heard that during the occupation in the early 'forties, these families had to make some tough decisions. Some

82

collaborated with the Germans, others even went back to Germany. But a lot of them resisted the Germans and were loyal to Poland.

"Around here, a lot of people have learned that you never know how long an occupation will last and who the next occupier will be."

We were almost back at Kolbuszowa. "See that cemetery? I remember visiting it when I was young. That's where my grandparents are buried. And their grandparents. I think there are Konefals there going back a couple hundred years."

CRACOW IS THE HEART OF POLAND and the Wawel Castle, in turn, is the heart of Cracow.

We were travelling in a rented taxi, complete with its owner-driver, Antek. The car was a ten-year-old Russian-made Volga. It stood out rather dramatically from the thousands of small cars on Polish roads and streets, many of them Polish-made Fiats. So heads turned whenever the Volga passed by. What visiting Russian bigshots were these? And when we would stop and the "Russian bigshots" were wearing things like yellow golf jackets and plaid pants, the local folks were totally confounded.

Travelling by car had a lot of advantages in terms of flexibility and exposure to the countryside. And it gave us a bit of a fix on Polish pop culture via the car radio.

I was anxious to hear some "real Polish polkas" so we tuned in early and often. Invariably, what we heard were such old Polish favorites as "Jambalaya," "Swanee River" and "Take Me Back To Hollywood." Sometimes in Polish and sometimes in English. Think about "Jambalaya" in Polish.

One station, in a bow to tradition, American tourists, or something else, used a few bars of a Polish oberek every hour on the hour—as part of its station identification.

When we arrived at the Wawel Castle, I had only a vague idea of the outline of Polish history. When I left, it was difficult to suppress a feeling of special pride of origin, the kind of chauvinism "absorbed Americans" decry.

What can you say about a country that has gathered its national heroes dating back 900 years and brought them to a collective resting place? What can you say about the place itself? Call Wawel Castle an impregnable fortress or a palace of Renaissance beauty and you've barely scratched the surface. Call it a Polish shrine and you're closer. Think of it as a rarity *anywhere* and you're right on target.

The place goes back about a thousand years. From the tenth century onward, Wawel Hill was the residence of Polish kings of the Piast Dynasty. They were the first to raise stone structures on the site. About 1020, during the reign of Boleslas the Brave, construction of a cathedral began. For about six hundred years, until Sigismund III transferred the Polish royal court to Warsaw, Wawel grew as the center of Polish authority and culture.

Just inside the main entrance of the Cathedral is the crypt of St. Stanislaus, the patron saint of Poland, who

84

died a political martyr in 1079. Along the aisles of the church are the sarcrophagi of kings dating from that period. Casimir the Great is here and so too, Stefan Batory (1576–1586) and Jan III Sobieski (1674–1696). In a tomb in the lower church, Jozef Pilsudski, the twentieth-century patriot, rests, as do other cultural and political heroes of the century.

On the north side of the cathedral stands Sigismund Tower, built in the fifteenth century. In 1520, the famous "Zygmunt" Bell was hung near the top of the tower. This twelve-ton instrument, cast by master Johann Beham of Nuremberg, required 10 people to ring it. The modern visitor can only marvel at the dedication it took to raise and operate "Zygmunt" in an age powered almost totally by human and animal muscle.

The Wawel *castle* itself is no less impressive. Built from 1507 to 1536 under the direction of Italian masters Francisco Florentino and Bartolomeo Berrecci, as well as Polish nobleman Benedykt of Sandomierz, the castle has been called a magnificent example of high Renaissance architecture. (Not until the early 1600s would Bernini go to work on St. Peter's Square in Rome.)

Cracow is the site of many other historic structures, all rich in tradition. We visited the Church of St. Mary's in the city's market square, and once again I was impressed with the depth of Polish tradition. St. Mary's was begun in 1221 and finished about 1330. To fully appreciate such dates, I had to remind myself that Christopher Columbus was born about a hundred years after the church's completion.

Polish history comes vividly alive for all Cracovians every hour when a bugle call, the Hejnal, is sounded from the tower of St. Mary's. Tradition has it that the bugle call was first played hundreds of years ago by a trumpeter-watchman to warn of an approaching enemy. According to legend, an ancient trumpeter was in the middle of the warning when a Tartar arrow pierced his throat and killed him instantly. Today, the hourly bugle call ends abruptly, in the middle of a note. Every Pole who hears it* knows what it symbolizes.

A MIRACLE CONTINUES AT CZESTOCHOWA. We witnessed it.

We visited this place Poles hold sacred as a high point in our five-day auto trip. We had spent time at the beautiful mountain resort, Zakopane, in the Tatra region of the Carpathian Mountains. And we had visited what to me was a wonder—the vast salt mine at Wieliczka, which for hundreds of years has supplied Europe with much of its salt. I now appreciate what "working in a salt mine" can mean and I'll never forget the amazing statuary and architectural structures that men have carved out of the underground at Wieliczka.

But Czestochowa is another dimension. This is the site of Jasna Gora Monastery, which was built in 1382 and contains the famous Black Madonna painting which Poles venerate. That veneration is based on legends that

*Every day at noon, all radio stations across the country broadcast the bugle call from St. Mary's Tower.

illustrate how completely the Catholic Church and Polish nationalism are intertwined.

It's believed, for example, that the Black Madonna icon turned the tide against the fourteenth-century Mongols who had swept across Europe. Ladislaus, the ruler of the region around Czestochowa, commanded that the painting be carried at the head of his armies. The Legend of Jasna Gora has it that when the painting faced the Mongols, a great darkness covered them; they grew confused, fought each other and were eventually routed. Ladislaus ordered that a monastery be built on the spot.

Another legend dates back to the seventeenth-century Swedish invasion of Poland, when the Swedes had overrun much of the country. It is believed that their progress was stopped and their fortunes reversed at Czestochowa by the intervention of the Madonna. Polish soldiers, inspired by the abbot at the Monastery, rallied against the Swedes. Their offensive, aided by allies, eventually routed the enemy.

We attended one of the twice-a-day devotions to the Black Madonna at Jasna Gora. What impressed me most was the almost martial air of devotion. At the outset, in military fashion, a trumpet sounded alert. And through-out the prayers and hymns, there seemed to be a fusion of nationalism and religion.

The miracle of Czestochowa, then, is the depth of devotion there *today*. The day we visited, there were hundreds of teenage pilgrims who said the prayers and sang the hymns with a devotion that I have not seen among young people in many years. There is, of course, an air of Eastern mysticism in the Polish liturgy. Or at least it seems that way to an American. There is more incense, more liturgical art, more shadow. But most important of all, there is more readiness to believe.

THE ENTIRE TRIP CAME INTO FOCUS late one night, as the five of us were riding in the country darkness. The Volga held us quite comfortably—Antek and Dad in the front seat, Aunt Sophie, Jerzyk and I in the back. We had had a decent dinner, a few drinks and were heading into the homestretch of the trip. It was well after midnight, the narrow two-lane "highway" was all but deserted, and we were mellow. Dad may have set it off when he said, "You know, I've seen more of Poland in ten days than I saw when I lived here for seventeen years. But soon it will be over."

Somone started to sing. I guess we were all ripe, because before long we were all into it. First it was a Polish folk song I had learned in the first grade, "Wszystkie Rybki Śpią w Jeziorze," ("All the Fish Are Asleep in the Lake"). Then a song I remembered my uncles having sung soon after they had come from Poland, "Ja Jestem Amerykanski Bum"*

It wound up, as it had to, with "Sto Lat" which,

* A prime example of "half-na-pół" language many immigrants resort to in their early years in America.

loosely translated, means "may you live to be a hundred, my dear one."

The five of us were nearing the end of something precious. Sophie was crying. Others were too.

There was one more stop to be made in the south of Poland before our return to Warsaw and then home. Even in the context of the most unusual two weeks of my life, this stop will always be the most vividly remembered.

CHAPTER TWO

WE WENT TO AUSCHWITZ. It is now a museum in the town of Oswięcim, a permanent reminder of ethnicity gone mad.

Yes, curiosity was a factor. After many years of hearing and reading of the Nazi butchery, to fully believe it there was a need, perhaps perverse, to confirm it—to stand in a place where it happened.

But it was more than that. What had been a shaky resolve to visit this place when we arrived in Poland soon became a compulsion. Because World War II and Nazi brutality to Polish citizens is still very much on the minds of Poles. It is engraved in the Polish psyche. It will not die easily.

We toured the "camp" where, according to the International Military Tribunal in Nuremberg, "more than four million persons perished" between 1940 and 1945. How can the mind grasp such a statement? How do you grapple with the enormity of it?

The prisoners were brought here from all over Poland and all over Europe. Many were brought simply because they were Jews, but many others were political prisoners, members of the intelligentsia, or other "undesirables."

We walked the halls of the barracks. Inmates stared down at us from endless rows of identification photos mounted on the barracks walls. In one photo a woman inmate weeps—and the visitor all but weeps in return. What warp of fate brought them to this place forty years ago? Why those people, at that time, in this place?

All the grim remnants are on display. Personal belongings looted from the prisoners—luggage, watches, clothing, eyeglasses and even dentures, gold fillings and hair. The inhumanly meager rations are illustrated. The rags of prisoner "uniforms" and the sleeping stalls more appropriate for animals are reproduced in detail.

The camp is haunted. From the time you walk through the main gate with its cynical greeting to prisoners, "Work will make you free," you are struck with the feeling that you are not alone. Something of those who died here remains.

For me, the feeling was strongest at three places. The first was the cell of prisoner #16670, Father Maximilian Kolbe, a Polish Grey Friar, who volunteered to replace another prisoner sentenced to death. The cell is in the basement of infamous Block 11, where the Nazis conducted their first experiments with Cyclon B gas to kill prisoners. Kolbe's cell is marked with a simple plaque. Fresh flowers are placed there regularly. The relative isolation of the cell helps you focus on what took place here some forty years ago—the simple, eloquent act of one man giving his life for another.

Just outside Block 11, the mind is assaulted by the "Wall of Death." Standing in the courtyard, you see it, thirty feet by twelve feet of brick. You are overcome with the thought that on this spot a life was taken by firing squad—not once, not several times, but *20,000* times. What dreams ended here? What blood drenched this soil? What madness was perpetrated?

And, finally, the gas chamber and crematorium. It is impossible to walk through the chamber where hundreds were gassed without feeling their presence. It is impossible to see the efficient "materials handling" system which moved corpses into the ovens and not wonder about the depths to which those who designed and operated these systems descended. Poles who lived through these horrors told me that some of the Nazis involved were on drugs or were alcoholics. That is small comfort for those who seek a grain of humanity in the men who ran these camps.

It is understandable that Poles will not let this die. Like many other sites in Poland, Auschwitz is "a monument of the Martyrdom of the Polish Nation and of Other Nations." Poles understand the dedication of the Jewish community in telling and re-telling the horror of The Holocaust. But they believe that a companion horror, the attempted eradication of Slavic leadership and enslavement of Slavic people, is not nearly as well told nor understood in America and around the world.

I was given official estimates of deaths of Polish citizens that surprised and shocked me. About 5½

million Poles lost their lives because of the Nazi "politics of extermination."* Polish government statistics provide this grisly breakout: Victims murdered in camps, executions, liquidation of ghettos, 3,577,000; victims of "bad treatment" in camps, malnutrition, disease, etc., 1,286,000; deaths outside of camps due to wounds, mutilations, excess work, 521,000.

Of these 5½ million Poles, a little more than half were Jewish.

In his "The Rise and Fall of the Third Reich," William L. Shirer has written at some length about the Nazi policy of eradication of Slavic leadership:

"Hitler knew very well what he wanted . . . : a Nazi-ruled Europe whose resources would be exploited for the profit of Germany, whose people would be made the slaves of the German master race and whose 'undesirable elements'—above all, the Jews, but also many Slavs in the East, especially the intelligentsia among them—would be exterminated. The Jews and the Slavic peoples were Untermenschen—subhumans. To Hitler they had no right to live, except as some of them, among the Slavs, might be needed to toil in the fields and the mines as slaves of their German masters . . .

"Hitler . . . had expressed it this way: 'The men capable of leadership in Poland must be liquidated . . . Those following them must be eliminated in their turn . . .'

*This does not include some 644,000 Poles killed as a direct consequence of military operations.

93

"On June 14 [1940] Auschwitz was officially opened as a concentration camp for Polish political prisoners whom the Germans wished to treat with special harshness . . ."

Quite often "removing Polish leadership" meant elimination of the clergy. There were instances of executions or enslavement of professors and university officials, such as the infamous "roundup" of Cracow University professors just after the fall of Poland, but more frequently such acts involved priests and bishops.

Polish government documents describe the German plan this way: "The extermination of the clergymen ensued from the precisely elaborated plans for the liquidation of Polish intelligentsia. In view of the large number of the Roman Catholic creed followers in this country, the Catholic clergy was a group of Polish intelligentsia which the occupier wanted to remove from public life . . .

"Out of a total of 10,217 priests, as many as 3,646 were imprisoned at German camps and 2,647 of them were murdered. As many as 836 friars died at prisons and concentrations camps over the period 1939–1945 as a result of the Nazi terror. As many as 1,117 nuns were imprisoned of whom 238 died in prisons . . . ; 3,780 nuns were expelled from their cloisters . . .

"The Roman Catholic Church hierarchy in Poland also fell victim to the Nazi terror. In 1939, when nearly the whole Chelmno chapter members were murdered, Bishop Konstanty Dominik was taken to Gdansk. Bishop Michal Kozal from Wloclawek died at Dachau in

1943. Archbishop Antoni Nowowiejski and Bishop Leon Wtmanski of the Plock diocese died in Dzialdowo in 1940. Similar fates of six other Polish Catholic bishops, as well as the head of the Polish Evangelical Augsburg Church and the Bishop of Vilnius, Lithuania, are also documented."

The World War II "resettlement" and enslavement has left equally deep scars among Poles. For the most part "resettlement" meant that Poles living on land desirable to the Nazis, mainly in Western Poland, were driven eastward. According to Shirer, "On October 9 [1940], two days after assuming the latest of his posts, Himmler decreed that 550,000 of the 650,000 Jews living in the annexed Polish provinces, together with all Poles not fit for 'assimilation,' should be moved into the territory of the General Government, east of the Vistula River. Within a year, 1,200,000 Poles and 300,000 Jews had been uprooted and driven to the east . . .

"It was an unusually severe winter . . . and the 'resettlement,' carried out in zero weather and often during blizzards, actually cost more Jewish and Polish lives than had been lost to Nazi firing squads and gallows. Himmler himself may be cited as an authority . . . :

'It happened in Poland in weather forty degrees below zero, where we had to haul away thousands, tens of thousands, hundreds of thousands; where we had to have toughness—you should hear this, but forget it immediately—to shoot thousands of leading Poles

. . . Gentlemen, it is much easier in many cases to go into combat with a company than to suppress an obstructive population of low cultural level, or to carry out executions or to haul away people or to evict crying and hysterical women.'"

So much for Nazi humanitarianism.

Often "resettlement" was simply a euphemism for the creation of slave labor. Although many concentration camp workers were forced to work on nearby farms and in factories, most of the forced labor from Poland and elsewhere took place in Germany.

Shirer puts it this way: "By the end of September 1944, some seven and a half million civilian foreigners were toiling for the Third Reich. Nearly all of them had been rounded up by force, deported to Germany in boxcars, usually without food or water or any sanitary facilities, and there put to work in factories, fields and mines. They were not only put to work but degraded, beaten and starved and often left to die for lack of food, clothing and shelter . . . In the East, when there was resistance to the forced-labor order, villages were simply burned down and their inhabitants carted off. Rosenberg's captured files are replete with German reports of such happenings. In Poland, at least one German official thought things were going a little too far."

Poles are like other people who have been victims of attempted ethnic extermination and enslavement; they want the world to remember. In an older case, Armenians still seek to perpetuate the memory of a million of their countrymen reportedly wiped out in Turkey in 1915–16.

There is a contagion in racial violence. The Nuremberg documents tell us that the virus of the Armenian massacre lived in Hitler. Just before invading Poland, he asked Goering, "Who still talks nowadays about the extermination of the Armenians?"

That virus must be expunged whenever it appears. And it has appeared throughout history. As Michael J. Arlen, an Armenian-American, reminds us in "Passage to Ararat:" "What of the countless other peoples who had undergone massacre and genocide: the Ibos of Nigeria; the Communists of Indonesia; the Hindus of Bangladesh; the Incas of South America; the Indians of North America; the Ukrainian peasants of the U.S.S.R.; the black slaves of Haiti and Guadeloupe; the Protestants; the Catholics; the Muslims; the Cappadocians who Tigran of Armenia had marched across the wilderness to his new capital; and all the rest whose names and stories were never entered, or entered vividly enough, in history books—for the list is surely long and ancient?"

As we were about to leave Auschwitz, we stopped briefly to watch a short ceremony. It was September 1, the fortieth anniversary of the German invasion of Poland. Members of an international youth organization had come to mark the occasion.

At the climax of the ceremony, a young man, the spokesman for the group, stepped forward. He offered a brief prayer and then a promise, "We pledge: No more wars. No more Auschwitzs."

CHAPTER THREE

WHAT WILL BECOME OF POLAND? Obviously, it's a question that interests millions of Polish Americans. And, since the momentous Polish worker uprisings of 1980, it's a question that interests Americans generally and people the world over.

Geopolitically, the country is, as always, crucial. The perennial buffer, it is the corridor through which many Warsaw Pact forces would have to pass in any confrontation with NATO. With its five-hundred mile border with the Soviet Union, and its two other land borders with Eastern-bloc nations, Poland is the strategic center of East Europe.

There's more. Here is a Socialist state which, while abutting its parent-ally, seems to be evolving a variant system tuned to its specific traditions, resources and needs. Here, perhaps more than anywhere on earth, Socialism and the Catholic Church have reached accommodation—admittedly an uneasy peace, one that could unravel abruptly. Here a Socialist government not only tolerates "the opium of the people," but watches it being passed from generation to generation. Surely, this is not what Marx had in mind.

Poland, then, could well be called a laboratory. In it, socio-political concepts are evolving that could have global implications. Like any laboratory, it can be a dangerous place. Mishandling any of the explosive elements used in the experiments could be disastrous. After thirty-five years of the experiment, the technicians seem to have the situation under control. But the test "species"—the Polish people—are a restless lot.

In 1980, the laboratory that is Poland almost exploded. The valiant shipyard workers of Gdansk—"moved to inaction" by high food prices and low wages—accomplished the impossible. Those workers and thousands of others all over Poland stopped work until the government granted major concessions—independent trade unions, the right to strike and media exposure.

NEVERTHELESS, THERE WILL BE NO "ROLL-BACK" SOON. Only a few years ago, there were many groups in America demanding "Free the Captive Nations!" Their ranks are thinnning as time and political reality take their toll. More important, there seems to be a growing realization that most people in "the captive nations" seek to improve their lot without risking violent confrontation.

In Poland, I found that people were quite consumed in trying to deal with their day-to-day problems. Not that ideology and nationalism are unimportant or obsolete. Back in Warsaw for a few days before we returned to America, I spent some time with several younger members of the professional class, discussing their views of the future of Poland and the world. These are people in their thirties, most of them journalists but also a few managers of government and commercial enterprises. They are Poles first, then participants in a certain political system. It is the only political system they have ever experienced.

The system has educated them and now expects return on its investment. These young, productive and promising citizens are not likely to be allowed to emigrate. Many wouldn't if they could.

A composite of their comments on Poland's recent past and its current situation is as relevant in 1981 as it was when the comments were made:

"Look, we know this country and this system are not perfect. We know a good bit about life in your country and the West in general. Of course, it has its appeal.

"But Poland is our country. If it is not as free as we might like, a good part of the blame lies at America's doorstep. Who was in a commanding position late in World War II and at the Yalta and Potsdam Conferences? And what did you do with that strength when it came to re-structuring Eastern Europe?

"We are the inheritors of that legacy. And unless there is some dramatic stupidity perpetrated upon us by the government or its allies, we are prepared to work out our difficulties gradually. So help us with trade, tourism and cooperation, but cool it on the 'captive nations' business."

CALL HIM "TEDDY", although that isn't his name. He is an editor of a leading Polish periodical.

A year before Polish workers, farmers and students were to press for economic and political liberalization —and almost a year and a half before Soviet and other Eastern-bloc troops were to mobilize on Polish borders —"Teddy" gave me vital insights into some of the forces that would bring Poland to crisis once again in 1981.

We had a leisurely lunch at the Warsaw Actors Club. He had suggested the club when I told him that I wanted to talk privately and at length to get his views of the future of Poland.

"Aren't you worried about talking politics in a public place," I started.

"Why should I worry?" he answered. "I have my idea of how personal freedom should be circumscribed. They (the government) have theirs. I apply my interpretation—which, of course, is quite broad—until they apply their stricter interpretation. So far they haven't done so."

I pressed on. "As a journalist, you are no doubt very sensitive to restrictions on freedom. Tell me about dissidents in Poland and how they are treated. For instance, just before I left America, I read about members of the Bratniak group being detained because they planned to hold a political meeting."

"Bratniak? Why do you single them out? They are just the tip of the iceberg, as you say. There are many such groups—and many individuals who question certain things without joining a group."

"Doesn't all of this dissent threaten the government? Couldn't it develop into a dangerous political movement?"

"In Poland, we are careful. There will be no violent movement here. The stark fact of life is that we live right next to the Soviet Union. As long as that is the case, fundamental change in our system will come only through careful negotiations and, of course, demonstrations where necessary."

"You mean there will be no 'Hungary' or 'Czechoslovakia' here? No suppression of uprisings?"

"You must understand a few things, my new friend from America. One: We are not under day-to-day control of the Soviets. It is more like a lurking shadow. We are evolving a type of socialism that seems to fit Poland, a 'soft socialism', as it were. Two: our dissident leaders are responsible people. We are not going to invite invasion. The danger is what you call 'wildcat' groups in the provinces. But by and large dissidents are careful and our government sometimes turns its head rather than risk confrontation. They know we are a fiercely patriotic people with certain, how do you say, 'hot buttons.' "

"What about freedom of the press here?"

"Obviously, your press and ours are quite different. I won't deny that what appears in my publication or in newspapers like TRYBUNA LUDU must be acceptable to the Party. I know of many stories that were 'adjusted' or dropped because they weren't acceptable. Usually, it's a matter of give-and-take between the editor and the party official. The censorship is total. But, of course, all of our readers know it."

"What about the underground press here? Is it dangerous to publish such newspapers or pamphlets? What happens when the identity of a dissident writer or publisher becomes known?"

"You've been seeing too many old American movies. The names are printed in these newspapers. Real names. The addresses are known. The government usually chooses not to make an issue, although it does make occasional arrests to set examples."

"Tell me about the Catholic Church. How is it able to maintain its influence?"

"After a thousand years, why not? There is nothing stronger in the Polish mind than the Church. It has been here through the city-state and the nation-state, through monarchy and republic, through occupation and partition. Everyone knows that there are now only two major institutions in Poland—the Church and the Party."

"But how are two such conflicting institutions able to co-exist?"

"Because, short of conflagration, neither can do anything about the other. It's a standoff. And maybe they don't have to be 'conflicting.' Some people believe that Christ was the first socialist."

"Are things changing here?"

"Yes. They've been changing for years. Now, the increasing contact with the West is making for more change. For example, more Americans are coming here, not just *Polish* Americans. And more Poles are visiting America. Student exchanges, faculty exchanges, just plain workers. Another thing: Never underestimate the importance of American public opinion to our government. We *must* export and America is a prime market for our products. If the government here did something that angered your people—like a brutal suppression of the Church—and you boycotted our products, it would be a disaster."

"What is the best hope for early change in the Polish political system?"

"I think it would be evolution, perhaps under a new regime, into something like what the Scandinavian countries seem to have, socialism with democracy. Right now, we have plenty of socialism but not much democracy."

It was time for him to get back to the office. We climbed into his four-passenger Polonéz and negotiated the busy streets of south Warsaw. As I began to leave the car at my hotel, we clasped hands and he said, "I hope to come to America soon. Let's be sure to pick up this conversation in New York."

THERE IS A FEELING OF ONENESS in Poland that is hard for an American to deal with. First, everyone is "Polish." There seem to be no immigrants here. No one speaks of being German Polish or Swedish Polish, as contrasted with say, Irish American or Italian American. It is an in-bred society. It is easier to speak of a "national will."

104

Almost everyone is Catholic. There were very few Jewish survivors in Poland after World War II and most of those emigrated to Israel. The Protestant sects have never really gained a foothold. So public religious ceremonies—Catholic ceremonies—that might give offense elsewhere are universally acceptable. As a child, I was taught that the church is "one, catholic, universal." Nowhere is this more true than in Poland.

I asked about religion among the Party and government leaders. Several times I heard the same answer. There is apparently an underground church among these people. They don't feel that they can practice the religion publicly, so they practice it incognito. When a child is born, baptism is arranged in a distant parish. Attendance at weekly mass is likewise often a matter of leaving town. Marriages are routinely conducted twice—one in the obligatory civil ceremony, another in church.

Teddy's commentary on the delicate balance between the Catholic Church and the government was brought home to me in this true story: The bishop of a medium-sized city in Eastern Poland recently became aware that his rectory had been bugged by the government. A friendly electronics expert did a "sweep" of the rectory for the bishop and found eighteen microphones. The bishop took the microphones down to his church and hung them in front of the main altar. The parishioners knew who had planted the "bugs." The bishop didn't have to make an issue of it. At the same time, the government was not about to enter a church to take them down. They hung there for the better part of a year.

So the balance is maintained. I was told that the Polish government has reconciled itself to the existence of a healthy, even flourishing, Catholic church (we saw churches being built in many of the cities and towns we visited) as long as it observes certain ground rules. Essentially, the Church is not to make comment in three areas: Polish-Russian relations, the inherent weaknesses of Socialism (although the failings of individuals in attaining Socialistic goals and ideals are fair game), and the desirability of international cooperation to build lasting peace (not likely to be attacked by the Church).

In the highly sensitive matter of Poland and Russia, we saw just how careful the Church can be. We attended Mass in Warsaw a few days before the September 1 anniversary of the outbreak of World War II. The priest who gave the sermon presented a stirring remembrance of September, 1939, focusing the congregation's willing attention on the valor of the outnumbered Polish soldiers and the efficient brutality of the German Army. He took us through the month almost day by day. But I listened in vain for mention of the mid-September Russian invasion from the East, an event all Poles recall with bitterness. It was obviously better left unsaid.

And in the amazing summer of 1980, it was the church hierarchy which sensed when the striking shipyard workers had gone far enough; when the risk of Russian military intervention had grown too great. Shortly after Cardinal Wyszynski suggested that the workers "cool it," the strike ended temporarily.

The vigor of the Polish Catholic Church was renewed

by the visit of John Paul II a few months before we arrived. Vestiges of his pilgrimmage remained—banners, pictures and even papal insignia on walls, in storefronts and, of course, to a much greater extent, in private homes.

The fallout from the Pope's visit is still being measured. But one thing was apparent to us—the visit not only consolidated existing support but was also an effective outreach to intellectuals and young adults. For example, vocations to the priesthood are up; there were reportedly twice as many, 2400, in 1979 than in 1978. This is a country which seems to have a surplus of priests (perhaps America will soon benefit from the surplus). And the number of young working-class people attending church-run "oases," summer camps, is also up considerably.

It was enough to give the government pause. Mieczyslaw Rakowski, editor of *Polityka* magazine, put it this way: "The Pope's visit has made the Polish Communist Party review many problems. But from the point of view of the development of our doctrine and the practice of socialism, this is not a negative development."

THE POLISH ECONOMY IS IN SHAMBLES. The events of 1980 made that clear to the world. "A few years ago, things were better," one of the Polish journalists had told me. "I really thought we were on the right track. Now, with all the shortages and the machinations of the government, I'm not all that sure."

The shortages are a heavy burden for most Poles.

Meat* is available only a few times a week. Lines start forming at dawn, several hours before the meat shops open; by mid-day the stores are sold out. Other staples of the Polish diet—butter, milk, eggs, vegetables—are more available but too often at prices that are out of reach for a good many people.

Consumer durables are available but expensive. A car can be purchased only after permission from the government and you can't make such a purchase more than once every three years. Of course, some people get permission faster than others.

Housing in some of the large cities is a scandal. It is reminiscent of World War II in this country—people making do in temporary housing, where the definition of "temporary" has been stretched well beyond its normal limits. We visited one young Cracow family of five living in a fifteen-foot-square room, with a shared toilet across the courtyard. They had been waiting for a modest apartment for six years.

It would be easy to explain all this away by pointing to the legacy inherited by the current regime. After all, pre-war Poland was no bed of roses. Inflation was rampant. The rigid class distinctions had not been adequately dealt with. And political leadership, after Pilsudski, had dissolved. In short, the country my father left in 1927 was not all that healthy by 1939.

Then came the devastation of the war. Poland lost

*Chicken, not included in the "meat" category, is a bit more available.

40% of its national wealth. Its industrial base was all but demolished. It had to pick itself up off the floor.

The trouble with this argument is that other countries with equally bleak prospects in 1945 have done so much better. Poles themselves, when they look at the prosperity and stable economy of West Germany, ask "who lost the war, anyway?" It is no comfort to remind them of the Marshall Plan and its positive effect on the West European economy. In fact, it's a point of abrasion, because it only serves to remind them of the Yalta and Potsdam agreements.

More to the point, perhaps, is that the Polish economy has seen better days as recently as the early seventies. But by mid 1980, Poland's debt had approached $20 billion in medium and long term loans, with $4 billion in hard currency due that year. It got to the point where the Polish government opened its books to "Western capitalist bankers" as a condition for discussion of new loans.

The foreign debt and need for hard currency has direct effect, day in and day out, on all Poles and, indeed, on their visitors. Poland must export as much as it can. The best Polish ham comes to America; Poles (and their visitors) must settle for inferior "szynka" or something called "cutlet"—a substance that turned up at every restaurant, its taste varying from succulent cardboard to delicious shoe leather. The only kielbasa we tasted in Poland was the result of Sophie getting to the meat shop at dawn and waiting for three hours. It was good, about the same quality as can be purchased in New York City any of six days a week.

Much more important, the shortages have led to a loss of civility. People push to the head of lines, jostle each other and sometimes even fight. (This is a universal human trait, witness the violence that occurred on lines at American service stations during the gasoline shortage.)

Things will not get better soon. In a few years, the Russians may not be able to supply oil to Poland. If the country has to buy from OPEC, there will be still greater cost pressures and trade imbalances.

THERE IS A RUSSIAN IMPERIALISTIC LID on Poland. Perhaps it's intrinsic to the socialist system. Perhaps any society with a highly-centralized government must function this way. I don't mean to judge whether the system is "right" or "wrong" for a country trying to work out the kind of problems Poland has had, and will have, for the foreseeable future. But to an American, it's all mighty uncomfortable.

Start with communications. Dad was watching television "news" for the third or fourth time when he turned off the set and gave his capsule analysis. "You know, it's funny. When I watch the news on television in America, if I didn't know about real life there, I'd have to say that just about everything is bad. Murders, fires, demonstrations, scandals. Here, it's the opposite. You watch television and everything is rosy. But when you look around and talk to the people, it's a totally different story. Who do they think they're kidding?"

I wasn't sure whether he was asking about just Polish television news producers or those in America as well.

Polish television and radio are state controlled. Big Brother decides what the citizens should be exposed to. There are some curious decisions. Poles are very big on "Kojak" and the "Flintstones." (I couldn't believe that Fred and Irma Flintstone could speak Polish, but there they were coming at us, handling some of the most difficult diphthongs on earth.) But when it comes to news and ideas, the government is predictable: only the socialist point of view.

Newspapers are the same. When a Russian ballerina visiting America decided to defect, the Polish papers reported it as an aborted kidnapping by the American government. They didn't tell their readers—and, of course, we didn't know until we returned home—that after careful soul-searching, the ballerina's husband had decided to stay in America. In fact, the Polish papers didn't even mention that she was married.

This censorship of the media* is the more passive form of government communication. The active form is "cheerleading" with banners in public places. We saw two kinds of banners. One was a celebration of the Socialist system, with special commemoration of the 35th anniversary of the government. The other took the

*Reduced somewhat after the 1980 uprisings.

form of exhortation to factory workers to meet production quotas. I couldn't help wonder how American union members would react to a government banner on their factory wall strongly suggesting more commitment for the greater glory of the state.

The deficiency of the system is apparent everywhere. It is a system without personal rewards. Theoretically, everyone is equal. But in a society where the best you can hope for is equality, there is a tendency to relax, to fall asleep. Nobody really seems to care about quality. Nobody seems to put out. On a visit to Poland a few years ago, the poet Antoni Gronowicz asked a high government official about this. "In our country," the official answered, "whether you work or not, you still get a guaranteed income. Only improved education and great self-discipline will develop a higher sense of responsibility in each citizen."

Admirable, but to a visiting American, it is the height of utopian idealism. More practically, if Poland is serious about attracting American tourists as part of its balance-of-trade objectives, it's going to have to do something about the attitude of the Polish people who serve these tourists. Even the low cost of a vacation in Poland isn't enough to offset the "I-couldn't-care-less" attitude among many Polish service workers. Only at the two Warsaw hotels managed by the Intercontinental chain was there "American" service.

Finally, there's the artificiality of the centrally-controlled economy. When bureaucrats decide the "right" prices and the "right" salaries—and the "appropriate" availability of goods and services—they take on the impossible. The free market isn't perfect, but it's certainly preferable to what we saw in Poland.

In Poland there is a black market in everything from Western currency to appliances to medical services. Why? Because when people really want or need something they will find a way to get it, even if an "omniscient" government has priced it out of their reach. "Getting it" may take the form of barter, supplemental payment or just plain stealing. This is the "Second Society" that has grown up in most East European countries. An Internal Revenue Services investigator would be in heaven in Poland, constantly tracing how it is possible for people on a strictly limited income to afford creature comforts that well exceed their income.

Ralph Nader and other "consumerists" would also have a ball in the centrally-managed economy. Where government is all powerful in the marketplace—where it *makes* and *maintains* the marketplace—"public be damned" is not just an irrational mouthing of an insulated capitalist, it's a fact. In Poland, if a product doesn't work, don't expect any solace from the manufacturer. And pollution control seems all but non-existent.

The "Second Society" has another function. It is largely the vine of forbidden fruit—Western books, music, clothing and other items the government would prefer that Poles be denied. Here college students may find the only available information on events like the 1939 Russian invasion of Poland or the massacre of Polish officers in the Katyn Forest by the Soviets.

This "private" sector has become so universal that officials usually close their eyes to it. Some even participate and benefit from it. Such "perks" that come with Party leadership are especially disillusioning to young Polish idealists.

IF AN EXPLOSION CAN BE AVOIDED—if Lech Walesa and other worker-leaders can keep their rank and file under control—change will spread steadily in Poland. It is, of course, long overdue.

Everywhere we travelled, we saw a grimness in Polish adult faces. The bright, smiling faces of the adolescent inevitably gives way to a brooding preoccupation by early adulthood. Something happens to these people not long after puberty. It is the system. It oppresses.

But new institutions for constructive, peaceful change seem to be evolving. The church is no longer the only only instrument for adjusting social grievances. Now, Solidarity has evolved as a genuinely independent representative of workers. Intellectual freedom, certainly not boundless, nevertheless is growing. And private farmers, who control about 75% of Polish agricultural production, are forming organizations which may some day evolve into a Rural Solidarity.

Whether these and other groups will prove long-lived and effective, no one knows. But Poles have already accomplished the impossible several times in the Post-World War II era. They have brought down governments without precipitating Soviet intervention. Gomulka is gone. So is Gierek.

In the long term, Poland will recover. Despite its current precarious position, Poland will recover because of the unique resiliency of its people. That resiliency hasn't changed appreciably in the more than 200 years since Rousseau took note of it:

"Poland, depopulated, devasted, and oppressed, wide-open to its aggressors, in the depths of misfortune and of anarchy, still shows all the fire of youth . . . Poland is in irons but is busy discussing means of remaining free and feels within itself the kind of strength no tyranny is strong enough to conquer . . . You prize your freedom and have deserved it."

CHAPTER FOUR

WAS IT WORTHWHILE, the trip to my grandfather's homeland? Absolutely.

Would I recommend it to others? Well, anyone who does it will have his own reactions, his own rewards and disappointments. Here's what the trip did for me:

First, it gave me a chance to do something with my father. And it was something important—for him and for me. He jokes about his age and how he doesn't plan too far ahead. But we were able to plan this together and then enjoy it. In recent years, we've seen a lot less of each other, grown apart physically, simply because of his move to Florida. After the trip to Poland, we're closer than ever.

Second, in doing research prior to the trip, I came to appreciate the immigrant experience more fully. My grandfather's experience has somehow come alive to me and, with it, the experience not only of other immigrants from Poland but from countries all over the world. I now appreciate a little more their difficulty with the language, the outright prejudice they sometimes encountered, their dreams for their children and grandchildren.

With that understanding has come the fuller realization that the immigrant experience still plays itself out daily in America; that our journey as a nation is a long way from finished.

The trip to Poland also satisfied the quest—the itch—that I've had for many years. It would be easy to go overboard on this. But like my grandfather, I'm more pragmatist than idealist. Even so, I feel a bit more whole for having seen the place where my father and grandfather and their forebears started life. I met my past in Poland.

I also acquired a deeper appreciation for Polish history and culture. The election of John Paul II helped spark that interest, but it was more fully stimulated by visiting Poland. A thousand years! I now understand why John Cardinal Krol, Polish American Archbishop of Philadelphia, usually a man of restraint, recently likened those who tell Polish jokes to "puppies yapping at our heels."

And the lessons to be learned by the trip to Poland are not all of the past. The contemporary Polish political and economic system—call it "soft socialism" or anything you want—should give Americans pause. The commonly-held notion that Socialism—we used to call it Communism without worrying about the distinction—is monolithic now appears naive. There are variations on their theme just as there are variations on the capitalist theme. And all continue to evolve.

A related insight from the trip: the growing interdependence of all nations of the world. We had better understand each other more than we have until now. We had better comprehend that the global village is upon us. International communications networks, especially television, make that certain; and the imminent increase in satellites and other new communications technology will confirm it.

More to the point, our economies are interwoven. The old east-west and north-south divisions no longer make sense. Some 85% of the world's population will live in "the third world" by the end of the century. Massive unemployment, starvation or repression half way around the world now reverberates quickly to our shores, witness the Iranian revolution. Foreign aid for economic development or agricultural production is no longer just charity. It's charity married to enlightened self-interest.

And the trip to Poland confirmed, as no other experience in my life, that it really is great to be an American. Despite all of our problems, doubts and mistakes, ours is the preferable option to all others. The author of "On Becoming American," Ted Morgan, an American naturalized citizen, has put it quite well: "Immigration is America's seal of success. . . . Remember this simple truth: This country is a success the same way that a Broadway show is a success. People are lined up at the box office for tickets of admission."

I returned to America with a new appreciation of just how important it is to have outlets for grievances. How necessary it is for a free press to keep citizens informed. How important are the institutions that contribute to a self-correcting society. And, perhaps most important of all, how the human spirit demands the opportunity for growth and upward mobility.

We had been away only two weeks. I was surprised by my emotions when, at 40,000 feet over the Atlantic, I first sighted North American land.

Discount the normal feelings about coming home after a long trip. The feelings were deeper—and more permanent. I was exhilarated simply to be in America again—and determined to share that exhilaration with others.

SOMEHOW, THE TRIP to the old country has sensitized me to things ethnic. Somehow, I now notice things that escaped me most of my adult life. Things like:

- The Brooklyn courtroom of Judge Mark A. Constantino, where 30,000 immigrants become naturalized every year—the largest "naturalization center" in the country. It is a room in which Judge Constantino recently concluded the citizenship rite for about 300 new Americans with simple eloquence: "America is you. Nothing, nothing is too far fetched."
- The intensity of people's feelings about their heritage —the critical importance of culture, religion and the tribal, racial or national identification in places as far apart as Iran, Africa, Yugoslavia and Canada. The

119

events of 1979 and 1980 in all those places, and others, demonstrated that people *care*—passionately—about their origins.

- The common threads, the shared experiences of so many heritages. Having reflected on the Polish experience, I better understand the psychology of the violated, the oppressed, the occupied wherever it surfaces. It is the psychology of many ethnic groups in many parts of the world. It often generates a passionate artistic expression, and, ironically, a fatalism. It requires lusty outlets—literature, drama, music and dance, and yes, even drink. And, in a way difficult for "absorbed" Americans to grasp fully, it generates a respect for authority, sometimes grudging, but no less real.

- An understanding of why many ethnics cling to their culture even after living in America for many years. It represents stability in a fast-changing society. Centuries-old values. Comfort, even warmth, from the familiar. And yet, over the generations, even this fades. And the very mobility of America provides the opportunity for absorption. There may even be global implications in all this. Historian Daniel Boorstin suggests that "if the United States can demonstrate anything to the world, it ought to be able to demonstrate that it's possible for people of different religions, and different ethnic origins and different races to live together, to marry each other, to enjoy each other's company, to delight in each other, and not be perpetually conscious of the racial barrier . . ."

120

IT WAS ONLY A FEW WEEKS AFTER OUR RETURN that Pope John Paul II came to America.

This Pope from Poland reminded Americans that they *are* all from somewhere else. In New York City, with the Statue of Liberty as a backdrop, he said the monument is "an impressive symbol of what the United States has stood for from the beginning of its history. This is a symbol of freedom. It reflects the immigrant history of the United States, for it was freedom that millions of human beings were looking for on these shores. And it was freedom that the young republic offered in compassion."

Then John Paul reverted to type. "And I see an inscription [in the crowd] in Polish, 'Niech Zyje Nam' (Long Live the Pope). I answer, 'Niech zyje Polska, niech zyja Polacy W Ameryce' (Long live Poland, long live the Polish people in America.)"

I heard that little speech on the radio while driving to a business appointment. And I reverted to type—with a lump in the throat and goosebumps all over my body.

ABOUT THE TIME AMERICA HAD ADMITTED SOME 50 MILLION IMMIGRANTS from all parts of the world—in late 1979—a brief ceremony was held on the shore of the great New York City bay where so many first saw America. It was a ceremony that should remind us all that the American journey is, indeed, far from ended.

Terence Cardinal Cooke, Archbishop of New York, was visiting the Mission of the Immaculate Virgin,

Mount Loretto, Staten Island. After enjoying a rendition of Christmas carols by 22 recently-arrived Asian "boat children," the Cardinal rose to acknowledge the children's performance. As he looked out at New York Harbor, he thanked the children and told them, "We are *all* boat people, you know. Our parents and grandparents came through this bay to get to New York."

Amen, Cardinal. No one has said it better.

"*Almost any pure material is weak, and many 'impurities' will do to make it stronger, i.e., to add to the pure material a kind of atomic grit—parts of a different roughness which stick in the crystal lattices and stop them from sliding.*"

J. Bronowski
"The Ascent of Man"